THE BOOK ON
SUPER
NATURAL
INCREASE

Experience Financial Breakthrough

& the Goodness of God

"in the Land of the Living"

Jeff & Patti Watson
LAS VEGAS, NEVADA

SUPERNATURAL INCREASE

CONTRIBUTING EDITORS:
Adele Visser of AVCA Creative Arts
Cell: +27(0)82-600-3601. www.visser969.wixsite.com/avca
visser969@gmail.com

Layout & Design:
James Kallas | james@dunamis.vegas

Dedication

I dedicate this book to my King and my God. He is my best friend, my Father, and the lover of my soul. I also dedicate it to my beautiful, sweet wife, "Princess Patti," who has loved me like the Lord does; my dear children Ian and Sheila, Shiloh, and Mckayla, who have shown me such love and honor and have accepted me as a father in their lives; and to my best friend, Dave, who, before his passing, walked and stood with me through fiery trials even and especially when no one else would.

SUPERNATURAL INCREASE

Endorsements

"I've observed Jeff Watson's life with joy in a friendship of eight years. I've watched how God has blessed his life, and become inspired by how he can take somebody from ordinary to extraordinary. His writing will change your life and increase your faith—especially faith for finances. It will give you a desire to follow the Lord, walking with signs, wonders and miracles. Jeff writes from experience. Even as I have been reading his story, I sense the presence of the Lord. It has increased my faith.

I pray that as you read, you too will be transformed with the burning desire to affect your family, friends and all whom you meet. I therefore highly recommend this book to every believer that wants to experience abundance and the move of God in the church and workplace."

Dr. Gershom Sikaala
Best friend of Dr. Heidi and Rolland Baker of Iris Global
United Nations Goodwill Ambassador, Philanthropist, Author, Actor
www.hollywoodmasteryclass.com / www.gershomsikaala.org

Jeff Watson's book, Supernatural Increase destroys the long-held religious beliefs that poverty is compatible with a life of faith. God is a God of Increase. Jesus said that I have come so that you may have life and that more abundantly. There is no lack implied this promise from the Lord Jesus Christ. Supernatural Increase, captures the spirit of divinely inspired increase. Get ready for a life of abundance as you stand on the truths contained in Jeff Watson's book.

Dr. Francis Myles
Global Thought Leader
Author: The Order of Melchizedek
Scottsdale, Arizona "This book is a gift from heaven and will raise expectations in the realm of believing and seeing God move in your life and finances.

"Imagine making a living by giving! Jeff and Patti have done just that and they believe every believer can be free of debt and live an abundant life.

This is not only a book about finances but it's the story of restoration and the love of God bringing two very broken people together into wholeness. Their testimonies are heartwarming and a powerful example of God's love.

Jeff takes us through scripture opening our hearts and minds to the truth of God's Word as he dispels the lies that so many have bought into. I have known Jeff and Patti for almost three years. I am honored to have them as close and personal friends. They live what is in this book every day.

I would highly recommend Supernatural Increase *to everyone. It is not just a book about finances. It's a book about faith, grace and the love of God."*

Pastor Al Patitucci
Co-Pastor Beverly Hills Foursquare Church (1995 - 2015)
Vice President - Awake Israel Ministries, Tel-Aviv Israel

Reading through these pages, I immediately felt a shift in the atmosphere surrounding my finances and heaven's economy. Having been stirred and ignited, I was challenged with each page to believe God from a deeper place of faith.

Jeff's passion to bring kingdom riches to earth through the hands of God's people is clearly displayed in his writing. It is a passion that is both contagious and inspiring. Jeff and his wife, Patti, are living testimonies of the power of heaven invading our finances and the freedom that can be found as a result. Their stories and experiences backed with biblical principles, truth and accuracy will forever transform the way you view your faith and finances.

This book will empower you to see the reality of God's desire to increase and bring us into the full manifestation of His resources. I believe you will receive insight into key areas of unlocking heaven's provisions through prayer and faithful stewardship.

Many who have been enslaved to poverty and lack will have thought processes changed and hearts reoriented regarding heaven's economy, kingdom prosperity and what that looks like here on earth. Captives will be set free to live from a place of abundance that flows from the river of relationship with the Father.

I sincerely believe everyone who reads this book with an open heart will find the mantle of prosperity and rest that is on Jeff's life will fall over their lives. I believe readers will be blessed as they discover living a supernatural, debt-free life is not only possible, but is the desire of God's heart."

Dr. Tony Robinson
Founder, Dr. Tony Robinson Coaching
tonyrcoaching@gmail.com

SUPERNATURAL INCREASE

Foreword

I've wanted to be loved my entire life. I've wanted a husband that would teach me more about God and the Bible. I have both and more in my husband, Jeff. My mother prophesied multiple times that I would marry a man who would help set me free from having to work. Jeff has blessed my life in every area including that one. I have been transformed!

I've never been happier. The church we attend is liberating. My every heart's desire has come to pass as we live, truly, from glory to glory. It is heaven on earth! Jeff is heaven-sent.

Jeff takes time out of his day every day to listen to God, a practice he has been doing for most of his Christian walk. He prays for every situation in our lives. He prays for others. Those who take his counsel, prosper.

Jeff likes to say, "What if you got everything you wanted?" He is the head and priest of our home. I am living a dream-come-true and I give God all the glory!

I know that what God has done for me, he can do for any one of his much-loved children, especially you!

Patricia Watson

SUPERNATURAL INCREASE

Contents

SUPERNATURAL INCREASE

Introduction

This book is the story of two phases in my life: one of total loss, followed by one of total restoration and supernatural increase.

> **ISAIAH 61:1 (NASB) SAYS:**
> *"The Spirit of the Sovereign LORD is on me,*
> *because the LORD has anointed me to*
> *proclaim good news to the poor."*

The word translated here as "poor" comes from the Hebrew *anav*. This Word does not just mean "poor" in a financial sense. It can also mean:

1. Depressed in mind or circumstances
2. Needy especially in sanity
3. Humble and meek
4. Afflicted and miserable

When I got down to literally nothing, I saw that there were only two choices:

1. Trust God and His Word, and then stand on it. Don't move. Just wait.

OR

2. Trust credit cards, borrowing money, and looking for other people to bail me out.

My wife, Patti and I, repented of trusting credit and decided to trust God. We have dedicated everything we own to God and, it turns out, He is a much better steward. Because we did this, He tells us what to do with our money.

It is my prayer and expectation that as you hear His Word of our testimony and see the supernatural works of God, faith and miracles will be birthed into your own life so that you can experience the supernatural increase God has already promised.

CHAPTER 1

My Story of Ashes

"You need an attorney."

Those words represent the beginning of the end of a long and painful phase in my life. Twenty-two years of marriage had come to an end, and my soon-to-be ex-wife had hired an attorney. I turned to a lawyer-friend of mine for advice.

"Jeff," he urged me, "if the other side has an attorney, you need an attorney."

"Great," I replied. "Know any free ones?"

Of course, he didn't, and I didn't have the cash to hire one.

The time had come. It was the day before initial court proceedings and I was still desperate for legal representation.

I had no idea how to get the money, but I knew the God who holds all provision; therefore, I did the one thing I did know how to do: I prayed.

By 3pm that day, someone had gifted me with $7,000 and I had hired my attorney.

That night felt like an eternity. I tossed and turned as stress, depression and anxiety seemed to close in on all sides of me. Was I going to have to take the stand? Would I choke under the pressure and scrutiny? What was I going to say? It was all I could do to pray through the night.

Finally, it was dawn. Narrow beams of sunshine streamed into my bedroom. The long, terrible night was over.

As soon as I got with my new attorney, I asked him if we could pray. I prayed and he agreed in prayer.

I wish I could say I led a powerful, triumphant decree over us and everyone involved, but the prayer was more like, "I need you Lord!"

Making our way to the courthouse, anxiety rose in me like an emotional acid reflux. I had butterflies in my stomach and was exhausted from being up all night.

But, God!

As soon as I took my seat in the courtroom, a deep peace overcame me. Jesus was by my side.

The judge announced our case.

My wife's attorney handed mine a piece of paper. I waited in suspense as he read it quietly.

Saying nothing at all to me, he then turned to the judge, announced himself as my legal representation, and moved for an extension.

The request was granted, and I exhaled.

The note accused me of deliberately refusing to work to avoid paying spousal support.

This could not have been further from the truth.

I owned a construction company. All through this season of marital trouble, I had continued to bid for jobs. In fact, I had bid on a ton of jobs, but for some reason, I simply wasn't getting the work.

The construction industry started to decline in 2005, and I was feeling the impact firsthand. My last job finished something like this:

"See these homes?" the company head asked me.

I saw them. My crew and I had built them. We were doing great work and right on schedule, contracted to build an entire community of these tract homes. I wondered where he was going with this.

"We are going to stop right there."

He pointed four lots down. Four more houses, and we'd be out of work. Just like that, everything changed.

For the next several years, I continued to bid but struggled for steady work and income. It was ironic: I built homes for a living. Then, one day, after the divorce was underway but before it was finalized, I returned to my own home to find the doors locked. For a long time after that, I had no home that I could call my own. I called my lawyer and said I was locked out, he reminded me: "You're not going to stay there anyhow."

He was right. A door had closed and there was no way to open it.

For the next few months, I stayed with friends and family. The work in my area of California had dried up.

Dave, my best friend, lived in Henderson, Nevada.

"There's a lot of building going on in the Vegas area," he suggested. "Why don't you come here and look for work?"

So, I did.

For the next seven months, I made my appearances in court as I couch-surfed from house to house, accepting the kindness of people I hardly knew. Some were complete strangers.

I had lost not only business, finances, my own house and family, but also friends, and even my pastor. I felt cut off and abandoned.

Before that season was through, I had moved nine times. By God's grace and because Jesus truly never left my side, I never slept on the street, but I was still losing hope and I told people around me I didn't think I was going make it. The Lord kept putting on my heart to let it all go and that He just wanted me to trust Him.

The Cost of Following Jesus

Jesus Was Hated Without a Cause

Jesus was hated without a cause. I also was hated by people but didn't understand why. I just wanted to serve my Jesus and do what He told me to do. One such friend of 17 years turned his back on me during this season, even though I had stood with him through his own divorce. In my time of greatest need, he abandoned me. The more I did what God told me to do, the more trouble I got into, and the more I was judged. I was not perfect by any standard, but I still desired to do God's will, no matter what. It seemed Jesus was the only one who loved me during this time. He stood by me no matter what and He did not leave my side.

You Will Be Rejected

Jesus told the disciples if they "reject you, they reject me." Were the disciples perfect? No, but they were His chosen vessels. Not being chosen isn't the issue. It's living for God and not for man that we have a problem with. Paul was not living for pleasing man, but being obedient to Christ.

> **GALATIANS 1:10-12**
> *For do I now persuade men, or God? Or do I seek to please men? For if I still pleased men, I would not be a bondservant of Christ.*
>
> This is Paul's Call to Apostleship. This man that is called by God, His Gospel comes from a revelation of Jesus Christ.
>
> *But I make known to you, brethren, that the gospel which was preached by me is not according to man. For I neither received it from man, nor was I taught it, but it came through the revelation of Jesus Christ.*

Revelation means to "take the veil off." God reveals Himself more and more, especially through the trials we go through. For it is in the trials that we turn to Him and find that He is a sanctuary for safety. He is my hiding place. Psalms reveals this treasure.

> **PSALM 91:1-2 (GOD IS OUR SECRET PLACE)**
> *He who dwells in the secret place of the Most High Shall abide under the shadow of the*

*Almighty. I will say of the Lord, "He is my
refuge and my fortress; My God, in Him I will
trust.*

Remember Jesus said:

MATTHEW 10:34-39
*"Do not think that I came to bring peace on
earth. I did not come to bring peace but a
sword. For I have come to 'set a man against
his father, a daughter against her mother, and a
daughter-in-law against her mother-in-law' and
'a man's enemies will be those of his own
household.' He who loves father or mother
more than Me is not worthy of Me. And he who
loves son or daughter more than Me is not
worthy of Me. And he who does not take his
cross and follow after Me is not worthy of*

*Me. He who finds his life will lose it, and he
who loses his life for My sake will find it."*

Will You Follow Jesus?

Let me try and explain the scriptures above (***Matthew
10:34-39***). You are to love your wife and your family. You
are also to follow Christ and do what He tells you to do. This
is the dividing line. There are a lot of people that have
prayed the prayer of salvation, accepted Jesus into their lives
but do not follow the Lamb wherever He goes. Look at their
lives and ask yourself where is the fruit? How are they living
and what cost have they paid? It does not cost anything to
get saved but following Jesus can cost you everything, even
your life. Are you willing to give up everything for Him?

When I was in this long seven year trial of losing everything, I asked the Lord what He was doing and He said, "I am giving you the desires of your heart and making you the priest of your home." I did not understand this at the time, but I do now.

Are you willing to pay the cost and keep doing what you believe what God told you to do? Even if no one agrees with you? Are you willing to put God first all the way through? In the next scriptures, Jesus is explaining you may not have a place to lay your head. You may want to do something that seems more important to you than what God wants you to do.

The Cost of Discipleship

LUKE 9:57-62
Now it happened as they journeyed on the road, that someone said to Him, "Lord, I will follow You wherever You go." And Jesus said to him, "Foxes have holes and birds of the air have nests, but the Son of Man has nowhere to lay His head." Then He said to another, "Follow Me." But he said, "Lord, let me first go and bury my father." 60 Jesus said to him, "Let the dead bury their own dead, but you go and preach the kingdom of God." And another also said, "Lord, I will follow You, but let me first go and bid them farewell who are at my house." But Jesus said to him, "No one, having put his hand to the plow, and looking back, is fit for the kingdom of God."

Again, consider if you are willing to build something without knowing if you have enough money to complete it. Are you willing to follow Jesus and consider what could happen?

Count the Cost

> **LUKE 14:28-33**
> *For which of you, intending to build a tower, does not sit down first and count the cost, whether he has enough to finish it— lest, after he has laid the foundation, and is not able to finish, all who see it begin to mock, saying, 'This man began to build and was not able to finish'? Or what king, going to make war against another king, does not sit down first and consider whether he is able to war with ten thousand men against an army of twenty thousand? Or else, while the other is still a great way off, he sends a delegation and asks conditions of peace. So likewise, whoever of you does not forsake all that he has cannot be My disciple.*

When you have given your life to Jesus, there is no turning back. I kept thinking of these scriptures when I was going through everything and they came alive to me. They comforted me and gave me understanding what Jesus taught. Most everything we go through in life gets down to this one thing, to serve the Lord and let Him be the Lord of our life.

CHAPTER 2

California Revival

During the years of unrest in my first marriage, I made a new friend. He thought he'd be visiting for a two-week vacation, but God had other plans.

How I Met Dr. Gershom Sikaala

Five Cities Vineyard Church in Arroyo Grande, CA had invited me to teach a weekly class, which for me had one purpose: teach others to hear God's voice. People came from across the city and region to attend.

After worship, many were sharing their experiences and testimonies. A visitor came forward. His name was Dr. Gershom Sikaala, a minister traveling from Zambia across the world to preach.

As he spoke, he began prophesying and, spontaneous healings erupted all over the room. What began as a simple meeting became an outpouring of the fire and Spirit of God. Dr. Gershom and I have been friends ever since.

America is Your Destiny

One day soon after that event, Dr. Gershom joined several people from our group as we went to minister to a girl suffering with vertigo. When we got there, we quickly discerned it was a spirit, prayed, and she passed out on the floor, completely delivered.

The love, joy and power of God gripped my heart as I saw God's will over Dr. Gershom.

"You thought you came to America for a two week vacation," I prophesied. "You have just stepped into your destiny. America is your Destiny God sent you here to bring a revival with signs and wonders."

Whenever you pray and believe you have received what you asked for, the scripture says you will have it. Sometimes, the answer to your prayer is housed within a movement, a revelation, a miracle, or a person. I had been praying diligently that God would bring a revival.

"I will send someone and I will raise up people for this," I heard God say.

I believe that Dr. Gershom was God's answer to this prayer.

Many Churches Open Their Doors

In a place where the doors seemed always to close if not slam shut to new or itinerant ministers, particularly on a Sunday morning, almost every church in the area opened their doors wide for Dr. Gershom. From that point on, I accompanied him all over the region and was given the honor and privilege to blow the Shofar as a part of ushering in the presence and awakening of God. Everywhere Dr. Gershom preached, people fell under God's power and experienced supernatural healings.

The 7 Nights of Glory

During one gathering, Dr. Gershom called for "seven nights of glory," and asked me to coordinate the meetings along the central coast of California.

I prayed for a venue. Again, God provided!

Shouts of Grace Church in Grover Beach invited us into their home for the first two nights. We spent the remaining five nights in a field at the Miranda Ranch in the town of Nipomo.

During one meeting, Dr. Gershom began gesturing like he was pitching baseballs. He pitched the invisible ball, and people thirty feet away fell over as if real fireballs of God had hit them! Many were healed, delivered and set free that night. People were laying out all over the floor.

One family — the whole family — received the baptism in the Holy Spirit with the sign of tongues, speaking loudly and boldly. Many people heard from God and spoke words of knowledge.

One lady had to be carried out after the meeting. She testified later that she went to heaven for twenty-four hours.

I blew the Shofar during worship, and a young man testified that he saw an angel come alongside me with a Shofar. As I raised up my Shofar so did the angel, and the presence of the Lord filled the room as angels filled the church.

People came from all kinds of churches—Mormons and Christians from various denominations, all just hungry for a touch from God.

The second night, in came a girl who had driven by the church earlier and thought it would be awesome to go to heaven. She did not tell anyone or even pray about it, but only thought it.

My friend Mel was helping at the altar and saw this girl lying on the floor. The Lord instructed him, "Don't touch her. She is with Me in heaven."

When the girl awoke, she testified that God had taken her into heaven while she was there on the floor.

Another man, who had lived for nineteen years with spleen damage, received prayer and left the meeting totally healed.

The weighty glory of God hit everyone in the room, touching many with supernatural healings.

The Fire of the Revival

Out in Miranda's Ranch, there was so much supernatural fire that one of the neighbors called the fire department. When the fire department arrived, they found no fire burning.

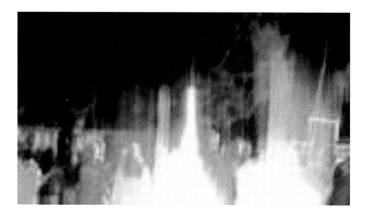

This picture was taken at the Miranda Ranch during one of the nights of glory.

Not only were the healings, wonders and miracles spectacular, but after those nights, a new church was birthed in the home of the Miranda family. Shouts of Grace Church grew to over four-hundred members.

HEBREWS 12:29
"For our God is a consuming fire."

HEBREWS 1:6
"Who makes His angels spirits and His ministers a flame of fire."

ACTS 2:3
"Then there appeared to them divided tongues, as of fire, and one sat upon each of them."

Give Me a Fire

Poem by Jeff Watson

Give me a fire that starts within
So hot I can't keep it in
The consuming flame that burns the dross
That I may proclaim Jesus on the cross
Let there be no friendly fear
No word of doubt to turn my ear
But totally in your love I go
That I may do the work you show
To be a true witness starts when you die
To think we can say the right words is a lie
After the death is the rising of the Son
When the world sees Jesus in you, the battle is won.

SUPERNATURAL INCREASE

CHAPTER 3

Under Trial: Supernatural Boldness

Notwithstanding this incredible revival and many great encounters with God, I eventually did find myself in divorce court.

When I entered the courtroom, I saw my entire family sitting on the other side, my pastor with them.

"I would never go to court and pick sides in a divorce," my pastor had once said. Yet, there he was with everyone I'd ever known and loved sitting, on the opposing side.

I was called to take the stand.

My attorney asked me what steps did I do to get work for myself, on my license or work for other people. I explained my efforts.

This was crucial to our case. I testified to the truth—that for the entirety of our marriage, separation, and divorce proceedings, I had never stopped looking for work.

When my attorney was done, cross-examination began. Under ordinary circumstances, this would have terrified me.

I flunked second grade. I held a C-average throughout high school. Without my mom's help, I never would have graduated.

As a kid, my dad used to grill me. Over and over he would ask me questions seemingly just to intimidate me. I would become flustered and unable to comprehend what he was saying. If I did try and respond, it was never what he wanted to hear—and that made him angry.

Into my adulthood, being on the other end of any kind of questioning made me freeze, stutter and say the wrong things.

So being cross-examined in a court of law should have left me with my foot in my mouth before I could finish my first sentence, but the presence of God overcame me.

Something supernatural happened. I knew what the attorney was going to ask before the questions came. Answers just flowed out of me. The judge chimed in and began questioning, too. That really should have done me in.

Nevertheless, dates, job descriptions, fees paid, names of people—information just kept coming as fast or faster than the questions.

I was amazed at the clarity and detail of my answers, and I knew this could only be God.

Matthew 10:19-20

"But when they deliver you up, do not worry about how or what you should speak. For it will be given to you in that hour what you should speak; for it is not you who speak, but the Spirit of your Father who speaks in you."

Once the cross-examination was complete, my attorney approached the judge with a 7 inch stack of papers.

"These are all records of Jeff Watson's past seven years of bids and jobs."

That stack of papers, plus the amazing testimony God graced me to give on the stand, disproved the accusation that I was plotting to weasel out of paying spousal support.

It was a great victory! I walked out of that courtroom with my head held high. My lawyer said that I was a very good witness. I told him it was God. He deserves all the glory.

Morning Prayer After the Court Victory

"Good morning Lord Jesus. Oh, what a great God You are. Who is like my God? In all this time, you have been faithful to me. You have done wonders and keep showing me that You put me up to this, because You back me up in every move.

Oh, You are faithful! You put defeat on my enemies' faces. They look away with discouragement because of the truth. They wanted to destroy me, but that was not in my heart for them. I was willing to give it all away. I was generous to them and they did not see it. My heart was always for their good. I have forgiven them from the well of forgiveness of how many times You have forgiven me and how deep that well is inside of me. I swim in the depths of my God's forgiveness. For I cannot count how many times You have forgiven me and how many times I have needed it. I will need this grace, forgiveness and the deep love You have for me now and forever.

I sought the Lord and He answered me and saw the anguish of my soul. You delivered me from my enemy who was too strong for me. You answered the cry of my heart. You delivered me from the snare of the trapper. You protected me from the fire. You shut the mouth of the lion. You gave me favor with a judge more than my adversary. This judge was harsh upon those who wanted to destroy me. He judged us with an equal weight, yet his gavel fell upon those who lifted their heel against me. You have delivered me, and Your kindness is always upon me. Your mercy triumphs over judgment!"

CHAPTER 4

My Friend Passes Away

At an Agape Church outreach in Oceano, California, Dave prayed over me more of a touch of God and to see Revival.

Dave and I had never met before that day. He could not have known that revival in my region was the constant prayer and desire of my heart.

Later, when God called me to Agape, we hung out all the time.

Dave and I shared a hunger to see people saved, healed and set free by the power of God. On street corners, in supermarkets, churches and restaurants, we loved to pray for people. God healed backs, lungs and knees. We prophesied. Countless received Jesus. We formed a ministry called The Two Witnesses. It was like we had always been best of friends.

Beans and Rice and Jesus Christ

Beans and Rice and Jesus Christ was part of a food ministry that did outreaches and held local events. Dave and I once helped them to organize a carnival and barbecue. We were like kids in a candy store as we helped Carol Ann organize the event Over one-thousand people were fed that day, and many gave their lives to Jesus.

A Spare Shofar?

"You forgot your Shofar!" Dave gasped as we drove to Fresno, California. He understood the power of blowing the Shofar, and how much it meant to me.

Peace and great faith filled my heart.

"God will provide a Shofar," I said.

When we arrived in the parking lot, I immediately spotted two men: one holding a Shofar, and the other holding two.

There is my Shofar that God has provided, I thought. All that was left to do was ask.

Moments later, I was holding that spare Shofar. we all blew our Shofars together.

One of the two men poured anointing oil over me and anointed me to blow the Shofar. Immediately, I fell backwards, but it was in slow motion, as if invisible angels were carrying me gently toward the ground. Wow!!!

Once I recovered and was back on my feet, I meet John and Chris.

God provided.

At the Rehab Center

"All I can see is white," Dave said. It was the presence of God.

Dave taught me to soak in God's presence. On one occasion, while driving to a rehabilitation center in Bakersfield, California with three others, a waterfall of God's presence continually poured over and immersed us for 3 hours. God was preparing us to touch a lot of hurting people in the place where we were going.

When we arrived at the rehab center, one man was instantly highlighted to us all. The moment we laid hands on him and began to pray, he fell to the ground, shaking like a leaf as God delivered him from a broken heart and drug addiction.

We needed little introduction after that and launched right into ministering to the people. Healings, miracles, and deliverances ensued and continued for the entire weekend.

On Sunday, the final day of our trip, a woman named Carol Ann shared her testimony.

As she spoke, the atmosphere shifted. The substance of faith became tangible. Healing scriptures flooded my mind supernaturally. I knew it was time to take action. The second I had the opportunity to speak, the word of the Lord burst out of me.

> **MATTHEW 4:23 (ESV)**
> *"And He went throughout all Galilee,*
> *teaching in their synagogues and proclaiming*
> *the gospel of the kingdom and healing every*
> *disease and every affliction among the*
> *people."*

I shared the healing scriptures that God put on my heart.

One was Exodus 15:26 – "I am the Lord who heals you," and other things God gave me to share.

We opened the altar, everyone came forward and for the next three hours, prayed and prophesied over every person that came to us. Many experienced instantaneous healing and deliverance.

Just Two Knuckleheads

Every Thursday, Dave and I ministered at a church in Paso Robles. One Thursday, we found ourselves standing in front of an empty building. The church had moved and not informed us; yet, there we stood, full of the fire of God. There was no way we were just going home.

"Show us where you have for us to go today," we prayed.

A Hispanic church around the corner came to mind. So I told Dave and off we went.

At first, we stood quietly on the side during worship; but something stirred in me that I was to blow the Shofar.

As I did, I had a vision. I saw the worship leader pulling on a rope connected to a bell in the air, and on the bell was inscribed the word, "liberty."

"What are you guys singing?" I asked someone nearby, as all of the lyrics were in Spanish.

He replied, "God give me liberty."

God was about to move.

"I know God sent you here," the head pastor boomed from onstage, and promptly handed me the microphone.

Of course, I had no idea what to say, so I inquired of the Lord.

God replied, "Just tell them how I have been using you two."

Remembering a recent day, I proclaimed the amazing works of God. God had given Dave prophetic words for three young adults out on the street. The kids were so moved, they immediately gave their lives to Jesus. As I shared this story, supernatural faith rose like a vapor all over the room.

Dave began to prophesy over two individuals. They sobbed uncontrollably.

I felt the anointing bring my attention to people who had tried to do ministry and nothing ever worked for them. About 17 men answered that altar call.

"These men never received the approval of their Father," God told me. "They have been bound because of it."

I told them what God had said, and we ministered to each man.

God's power swept over us. My own body shook as I wept. I could feel the work of the Holy Spirit liberating them, just like they had asked Him to do in their song earlier, God give me liberty.

As God's presence touched every person and the miracles continued, Dave would say, **"We are just two knuckleheads wanting to serve God.** Would anyone believe how God would use us?! If you let Him, Come out of your comfort zone and He will use you, too."

Hearing Accurately

Dave and I went to a church in Nipomo, California, The pastor of the church, who is a prophet, said to Dave "You are a walking revival."

This was my dear friend, and I knew it to be true about him. Everywhere Dave went, people got blessed in the presence of God. He heard from God all day long and had many heavenly visitations.

Once, while working on a job site together, I told him we needed to organize the tool shed. He stopped me.

"No," he said, "not today. Today, we have more important things to do."

Then he said something about "a lien" and money. I didn't know what in the world he was talking about, so I just kept working.

"Look," he said, holding my phone up to me a few minutes later. There was a voicemail.

"It's important," he assured me, but neither one of us had heard the message or had any idea who left it.

I knew my friend well enough, so I stopped what I was doing and listened.

Not long before that day, a client had stiffed me on a job. The message was from a real estate agent calling to make sure I got a lien on that job so I could collect payment. Dave was right! We had more important business that day.

On another occasion, Dave was taking an online college course to become a licensed counselor. To complete the course, he had to pass his exam. Most people would be cramming day and night just to pass the test, but not Dave. He did not read any of the materials. Instead, he would pray and then take the test. Crazy, you think? He got straight A's!

God not only helped him with all the answers, but also gave Dave prophetic words for every person in the online class, including his professors. They all marveled how someone they had never seen in person could have such insight concerning their lives.

Through Thick-and-Thin

Dave and his wife were experiencing serious challenges in their marriage, but his heart for his wife never faded. Even on that rocky road, he refused to take off his wedding ring, continuing to believe that it would eventually work out between the two of them. He told me often how much he loved his wife, that he wanted no other woman, and that he could never stop loving her. I was the closest person to him and I can say without question that he was always faithful to her.

His kids were the pride of his life. He spoke constantly about his son, Zack, "the incredible athlete," and his beautiful daughter, saying, "She has my heart."

Dave would do anything for his kids. When he hardly had money for himself, he spent it on them. He was that kind of father.

Up for a Fight

Dave needed a bone marrow transplant because his body had stopped manufacturing his own blood. His sister, Betsy, donated her blood and bone marrow—a terribly painful procedure, but a sacrifice she was more than willing to make.

About a month-and-a-half later, Dave's body began rejecting the new marrow. He was in unbearable pain.

Many times, I asked him whether he was still up for the fight, and he always said, "Yes! I have not given up!"

He never did give up.

Whenever he was asked what he was willing to do to stay alive, his response was, "Everything!"

One day, his blood pressure dropped to 49/35. The doctor informed us that this would likely lead to cardiac arrest.

But Dave wanted to live!

I put him on a prayer chain, and guess what happened? His blood pressure miraculously jumped back up to 109/80.

It was a great victory and gave me hope, but in time, Dave's health continued to dwindle and, eventually, he was put on life support.

I Release You

Dave passed away while I was in the midst of court proceedings for my divorce. It was already such a hard time, and his passing made it harder. Losing him provoked many questions in my heart, and though I could not understand why I had to suffer so much loss in one time, I knew that God was with me. In fact, God stayed so close to counsel and guide me during Dave's last days.

In the final week of Dave's life, the Lord spoke to me about releasing him.

"If You want to take him, You can," I prayed.

Of course, I knew this was not my decision and the Lord did not need my permission. The time of Dave's passing would be between Dave and his Father, but it was powerful for me to set him free and accept with my heart that if Dave wanted to be with the Lord, I would love and support him even in that.

"I release you."

The day before his family was scheduled to take him off life support, I went to my best friend's side.

That night, I had a vision of Dave with the word "memorial" under him.

God had also spoken to Dave's pastor, who told me she clearly heard God say, "Dave is with Me."

Still another pastor, Karen Green, called to tell me that God had spoken to her about Dave as well.

"You can quit praying for him," she told me. "He said he is tired and he doesn't want to stay."

Others heard similar things from the Lord shortly before he was taken off the life support.

I was there with his pastor when it happened. Dave was no longer there. His body became a Dave Slocum shell. Dave was already with the Lord.

A Visitation

After his passing, I asked God to speak to me. I also asked to hear from Dave, who I believed was now in my "cloud of witnesses".

The Lord answered me… and so did Dave!

THE LORD:

"Son, I am not the God of the dead, but of the living. Dave is with Me. He has no pain, and he will never feel pain again. I am his God and he is My son and we will be together for all eternity. Yes, son, he is with Me and he is standing by My side forever. He told me he was tired and he wanted to come home. So, I welcomed him home, for I have prepared a place for you all to enter eternity.

No more tears, for I am with you. Your friend's name is written in the Book of Life so that he may enter heaven, his final home.

Son, tell Dave's family to believe in My Son, Jesus, and what He did for them. He died for all of you so you can come into heaven to be with Dave. Tell them not to miss this free gift of eternal life. It is for all the family—all those who are far off, and as many as would believe."

> **JOHN 3:16**
> *"For God so loved the world that He gave His only begotten Son, that whoever believes in Him should not perish but have everlasting life."*

> **JOHN 15:13**
> *"Greater love has no one than this, than to lay down one's life for his friends."*

ME

If you're reading this today, and you haven't yet, will you accept Jesus today like Dave did? Jesus died for you. Your only assurance of eternal life is to believe in Jesus and what He did for you.

DAVE:

"Jeff, I am here. I love you, my brother. I heard you the night you released me. I was concerned you would not let me go. I know you serve our King, and that you always do what is right for others.

It is awesome here in this place! Everything is unbelievable.

Tell every one of my family that I love them, and to accept Jesus as their Lord so they can come to where I am.

I was so tired, Bro. I couldn't do it anymore. I hoped you would understand my heart. I will do what I can from this end.

Also, this is the only time I can talk to you for it is forbidden for those from the earth to talk to the dead. Tell Mom I love her. Don't cry, Jeff. You will always have me in your heart. Tell Kenny he is my best friend and tell Mckayla that she is a princess. Tell Nick that God is with him and tell Shiloh that he is a man. And you, Jeff, my brother, there is no one on the earth I love more than you. You believed in me and stood by me until the end. You are a faithful man of God and you are a faithful friend. When everyone stood against me you stood by my side. I love you, my brother, and you will see me again.

Bye for now. You will prosper like never before in this 2012 and for the next seven years. So, store up everything you received and give to the poor. Especially, give God to the people.

"That's all for now. Bye, until I see you again."

The Third Time I Went to Court

About six months later, the night before my third court appearance, several church prayer groups were praying on my behalf. This time, I slept soundly all through the night.

While it was still dark, I awoke refreshed, climbed out of bed and made my way to the stunning Morro Bay Rock to worship God.

While there, I had a vision.

I saw myself in heaven, and God showed me the Baal worshipers who were cutting themselves.

"See!" God said to me. "Those who serve other gods hurt themselves but look at Elisha."

Elisha was there, praying, when fire came down from heaven.

"Ask of Me what you want, and I will answer with fire."

I asked that I would be granted a divorce that day in court, and that I would not have to pay spousal support.

Later, I prayed the same with my lawyer. We arrived early together.

As the others arrived, my lawyer suddenly got an idea and made a proposition to the other attorney. When he came back to me, he had arranged for a settlement. I agreed with the offer, and so did she.

The court opened for session and the judge entered. My attorney informed the judge of our agreement. The judge asked whether these things were true. We affirmed it. He finalized the divorce right then and there. God gave me what I asked for before the courtroom had ever opened!

47

God Provides a Buyer

In keeping with our agreement, I had to sell all my construction equipment and pay off the debt from my business. I was already living in Nevada and needed to do this quickly, but it could take forever to sell everything piecemeal. It's not every day you meet someone who is in the market for thousands of dollars' worth of used construction equipment all-at-once.

I prayed for God's help, and then felt the unction to call my friend, Ty, to see if he knew of anyone that would like to buy.

A little while later, he called me back. He'd a found a guy who wanted it all for exactly the price I needed!

I required a miracle, and God gave it to me. The money from this sale helped to pay off the construction debt.

Great Loss

This was a time of great personal loss for me. Losing my marriage, six kids, three daughters-in-law, one son-in-law, and ten grandchildren was heart-wrenching.

I also lost my construction business and the income of that business. My reputation with people was impacted. I was in deep debt. To meet my agreement with the court, I had to relinquish all of my construction tools. I literally lost everything but my truck, some clothes and my computer. I was homeless for many months, sleeping on people's couches and staying in friends' homes. Over the course of that year, I moved nine times. My best friend and ministry partner, Dave, passed away and I missed him terribly. I constantly wondered how I could possibly make it through all this.

Beauty from Ashes

Then, one day, God came to me and asked, "What do you want?"

"I never wanted to be divorced," I told Him.

I desired a wife!

The Lord replied, "When it is time, I'll give you a new wife who will be your heart's desire, who will honor you, love you, and be submitted to you. Also, you will be in a powerful church that does not play games with my anointing."

I was pretty specific in my request to the Lord. I asked for my wife to be 5' 5", athletic, thin, with a beautiful body and face; who is so in love with Jesus and who loves His glory. I wanted her to be smart, loving, kind, giving, and a good steward over money, willing to give things up for the gospel. I wanted a woman who would be in love with me and trust me; who would follow me as I follow Jesus; who would not be ashamed of intimacy but desired me as I desired her. We would pray about everything and she would hear from God as well. I wanted someone I could trust and with whom I could share in all the blessings that we would share ministry together, and she would have her own ministry as I have mine. I prayed that we would each have our own relationship with God, and that we would be happily married—for life.

Remember when I said I got specific? I also asked that she would not want a TV in our home. Our time would be spent with God and with each other and we would pastor together.

After I met Patti, the Lord spoke to me, "My Son, Patti has had seven-plus years of hard times, and you being in her life will turn that around.

She, too, has had all kinds of oppression. She, too, had let everyone else have their way, never fully receiving the desires of her own heart.

Now, I want this flower to blossom and come into full maturity.

Son, you have been praying for a new wife and a new family and this is what I have brought you.

This family has not had a Christian man or an example of a godly father. You are it."

God's Calling in Trials

God spoke to me clearly:

"Son, write down the good days and focus on the many things that are coming, for I will have My way. As the old fades away, the new is coming. There will be so much breakthrough that it will be overwhelming and you will not be able to contain it. It will be like a runaway snowball that is rolling down a great mountain.

It starts down the hill small, but by the time it reaches the bottom it will be almost the size of this great mountain. Son, I am speaking of momentum, blessing and breakthrough, with nothing holding you back.

Yes, I have called you to full-time ministry and you will not have a regular job. Your wife will also be by your side in full-time ministry. You will have a house paid-for and you will be debt-free. It is time to move in My authority and power in this region. It is time to be unhindered in all that I have called you to do.

Son, let your license go. Let liability insurance go. Let workman's compensation go. You are no longer in construction. Burn all bridges, for when I call someone into full-time ministry, I will pay. I will bring it any way I want and I will move many hearts to give and to contribute to your calling, which is the work of the Lord.

I have heard your prayers! Don't you know that these are My prayers and My plans for you and Patti? So, shut all doors that don't lead into ministry. Son, do not be concerned with the courts and what is going to take place. Remember, I told you that I granted your request. It is done. The devil wants you to keep being concerned, but I have spoken and you win!

The church I am calling you to will be known for apostolic authority, for power, and for prophecy that will influence the world. Those who have judged you for so many years will moan because of how far off they were. They will recognize how much they were holding you back from the fullness of what I wanted to bring into the Central Coast through you and through the people I have connected you with. I have just moved that calling to Nevada, for that calling is *in* you. When everything kicks in, you will be astounded with what will happen. Son, you have not seen anything of what I am going to do.

Son, be quiet about the marriage and the church. Let My reputation through testimonies and acts of power, authority, and prophetic words that will come forth from this church be the voice that people will hear."

CHAPTER 5

How God Answered

Patti and I began walking out and fulfilling everything God said from the start. On our first date, I took her to the Hoover Dam in Boulder City and we just hung out. I fell in love with her instantly. She was not just beautiful but had a gentle heart and a quiet spirit. The loving way she acted towards me made me feel amazing. We wanted to do everything together. At the writing of this book, we have been married for over five glorious years.

Patti is a true helpmate. She stands with me faithfully and believes through every trial.

In my previous marriage, I felt alone, like I had to do everything on my own. If not for God bringing Patti into my life, I might not have recovered from that season of great loss. Her love and support were like the rock of Christ to me. Over and over, she helped me move forward rather than get stuck in the weeds of the past.

It is possible for decades of wounding and pain to be healed in a moment. That has happened to me many times since marrying my wife.

One day, I needed to remove a heavy toolbox from my truck. Before I even began lifting it, Patti jumped up onto the truck bed and started to unload it, just to make it lighter.

Never mind the weight of the toolbox; the weight of years feeling alone and unsupported suddenly lifted off me. All I could do was weep. Patti is a blessing in the big and the small, often without me ever having to ask.

Patti was divorced after sixteen years of a bad marriage. As we came together and our lives became one, we talked about everything we could think of regarding our past. We talked about the hurts. We talked about our abusive childhoods and our failed marriages. We talked about it all and hid nothing. As painful memories surfaced, we would take turns holding each other and crying. We would speak and pray forgiveness over everyone who had hurt us. Through that healing and forgiveness, we knew we could truly move on and move forward into our new life together.

What the Lord Told Me

"Patti has a warm heart, but she is going to believe in Me more than ever before because of how I am going to bless you. You will be able to do all of the things that you two have desired for so long—some things for all your life.

This marriage is inspired by heaven, for everything you have been missing in a wife is found in Princess Patti. Yes, I have ordained this marriage and this is the one to marry. Son, this is only going to get better and better. Your love for one another will only grow. As you continue to bring Me into every part of this relationship, I will bring the supply of love you need for each other. There is no end to the supply of love and no limit to the depth of this love, for I am an unlimited God and there is no limit in Me. Keep bringing Me into everything in your life.

Pray for Patti, for she is your wife to be. You two will minister together. It is my heart for you two to get married and to spend a year to know each other. I know this seems like a slow start. Keep believing. Stay in the realm of faith.

I am honoring you because you have honored Me. I have promised that a hundred-fold blessing is coming. You truly have left everything to follow Me. This will be a blessing in every way. Yes, you can say you have hit the jackpot of heaven...777! Get a bucket, Son. Yes, you will see these three children, Ian, Shiloh and Mckayla serve Me with their full heart."

Our family vacation

Patti and I in Hawaii

CHAPTER 6

The Adventures Of

Princess
Patti Watson

by Patti Watson

When I was growing up as the youngest of seven kids, my home life was anything but peaceful. The one family vacation I can remember, my dad got drunk on a camping trip and my mother ended up driving all of us kids home without him. I was traumatized. I was terrified that bears were going to get my Dad!

From that point on, my family did not go on vacations. This was very disappointing to me. My parents eventually divorced when I was eight years old, but it had always been a desire of mine to take a trip to Hawaii.

I was married to my first husband for a difficult sixteen years. We could never agree on anything. We had two children, Shiloh and Mckayla.

> **AMOS 3:3**
> *"Can two walk together, unless they are agreed?"*

In that marriage, I thought about this scripture often and wondered whether it was indeed going to be the story of my life. I felt unloved, unheard, and that my happiness was of no consequence.

When Shiloh was 8 years old, I asked him to agree with me according to this one:

> **MATTHEW 18:19 (NLT):**
> *"I also tell you this: If two of you agree here on earth concerning anything you ask, my Father in heaven will do it for you."*

We prayed this frequently and, one day, I asked Shiloh to agree with me that God would give us a Hawaiian vacation.

A Sad Christmas

Shiloh's father would frequently lie to me, and we had been separated more than once. At this point, we were reunited for about a year after one such separation, and I warned him not to deceive me again.

It was around Christmas, 2002, and he was supposed to get paid from a job. I asked him point blank. He looked directly into my eyes and said no, he had not been paid.

A few days after Christmas, I found a bank deposit slip in the amount of $450.00.

He did get paid but had lied to me yet again.

My kids were ten and eight years old at the time, and because my husband was in the habit of using our family's income for his own exploits, our children had no Christmas presents that year.

That New Year's Eve, he came home drunk. We got in a fight. He got violent. We had the police come and he was arrested for domestic violence in front of minors.

He divorced me shortly after that.

On November 7, 2006, I told God I wanted restitution for the loss of being dishonored in that marriage and wrote down everything I desired. Then, I said, "God, *you* do this."

June 2, 2012, I married Jeff.

Jeff often says that God blesses unity, and with him, I have seen and experienced this blessing many times. In January of 2014, Jeff surprised us all.

"Let's take all the kids to Hawaii!" he proposed.

My mouth dropped. I had never told Jeff of my lifelong desire to go to Hawaii. On May 19, 2014, I left with Jeff, Shiloh, Mckayla, and Ian and his wife for Kauai to experience ten amazing days in paradise.

While on our vacation, we were with Shiloh celebrating his 22nd birthday, when he said:

"Mom, three days ago God reminded me of what we asked for when I was eight years old."

Again, I was stunned. I had forgotten of that day many years earlier when we prayed, asking God for a trip to Hawaii. God never forgets! To God be all the glory! He is such a good God, and He cares about what is in your heart. He promises:

PSALM 84:11
For the Lord God is a sun and shield;

The Lord will give grace and glory;

No good thing will He withhold

From those who walk uprightly.

My Son Hears God

Shiloh was eight. He had taken ill and I kept him home from school. As the day progressed, he started to feel better and asked if I would buy him a pair of new shoes. On our way to the store, he asked if it would be okay with God to get one of his ears pierced.

"Shiloh," I replied, "you will know right here."

I reached over and put my hand on his tummy. His face lit up.

"Oh mom! When you put your hand there I felt God come in!"

From that moment and for the next day-and-a-half, Shiloh clearly heard God and conveyed everything he heard to me and his younger sister, Mckayla. He heard so much that I had to get a notebook to write down everything the Lord was speaking to him!

My Prayer List: God of Restoration

God's Word says that He is a God of restoration. On November 7th, 2006, I asked the Lord if He would make up for the loss of sixteen years. I wrote down everything I wanted:

1. Someone I could trust, who would love my kids as much as he loves me!
2. A home with a pool and beautiful landscaping
3. New living/bedroom furniture
4. Buy homes for investment
5. Family vacation in Hawaii
6. Car
7. Debts paid
8. Braces for teeth
9. Nothing missing, nothing broken
10. Happy, saved kids
11. House on the beach

I wrote my list out and put it in my prayer notebook. It wasn't until two weeks before we were to leave for our vacation in May of 2014 that I opened the cupboard door and saw that notebook.

Eight years after its writing, I was stunned to see how many things God had done. I did not realize all the answered prayers. When Jeff got home I showed him the list. We were amazed together.

Now that my Father has done all the things I asked for, I am dreaming for bigger things and asking for bigger. I don't want to ask the *King of Kings* for little when He paid the highest price to give me everything.

Retired

I was living in Santa Maria, California when I attended a "Rich Dad Poor Dad" weekend seminar. One couple that spoke told of their many assets, which would allow them to retire by the age of fifty-five. They looked about my age, so this got me thinking.

While driving home from the meeting I told God, "That's what I want! I want to retire at age fifty-five. I want to enjoy my life. I don't want to work like a slave till I am sixty-five and beyond."

Now, in the natural, I had lots of debt and was receiving unemployment. I didn't have a penny in my savings and I was only three years away from fifty-five. How was God going to answer this impossible prayer? I didn't care! It wasn't up to me to make it happen. It was up to God to fulfill His promises.

> **DEUTERONOMY 6:11**
> *"I will give you vineyards you did not plant!"*

I had been driving public transportation for two years and was fed up with the job. Jeff wanted to go to Fresno for the weekend, so I put in my request for the time off. That day, when I showed up for my route, the supervisor approached me:

"I am sorry I could not get you Thursday off."

They had given the time off to another driver.

I was at the end of myself! I put in for a sixty-day leave of absence and drove to the stop where I was to relieve a driver and take over the shift.

But, God!

Before I could begin my shift, another driver interrupted:

"Would you like me to take your route? Mine just got canceled."

Of course, I replied with a resounding yes!

God made sure I got those days off after all, and Jeff and I were able to leave for Fresno.

Sunday, on our way home from the trip, I broke the news to Jeff that I had taken a sixty-day leave of absence. He wasn't fazed one bit.

"No problem," he said.

Sixty glorious days later, I had no desire to return. Jeff and I felt released from it, and I never went back to work another day in my life. Now we minister full time, and we haven't looked back. Glory to God.

God Lengthens My Leg

For my entire adult life, I had one leg shorter than the other by half-an-inch. Because of this, I had to visit a chiropractor every few months for an adjustment. One afternoon, Jeff asked me to sit down on a chair and instructed me to raise my legs. Clearly, one leg was shorter than the other. He commanded my leg to grow out.

My eyes nearly popped out as we watched the shorter leg become the same length as the other! It was a true miracle. My legs have been the same size ever since. Glory to God! I don't have to try to adjust the way I stand any more, and my hips are straight.

Redeemed from the Curse

I started listening to the teachings of Kenneth and Gloria Copeland in 1982. They taught me how to find a promise in the Bible and stand on it until it came to pass. I have seen this truth manifest repeatedly in my life.

In 1977, I was expecting my first son, Ian. I did not know how to believe God in His Word, and having Ian was very painful. In 1992, I was expecting Shiloh. I was attending a weekly Bible study that my mother was holding at her house, and I asked Myrtle, the woman teaching, if women could have a pain-free child birth.

She said yes!

I wrote down all the Bible verses I could find pertaining to childbearing. When I was done, I had almost a full page. I read those scriptures every morning of my pregnancy. When I went to the hospital to have Shiloh, I did not use any pain medication. On a pain scale of 1-10, 10 being the worst, having Shiloh was a 1—so much easier and just by standing on God's promises.

I know beyond a shadow of a doubt that God's Word works. It transforms us from the inside-out. Standing on His Word continues to work for me, and it will work for you too.

Debt Free

In January of 2003, I became a single parent. By 2007, I had accumulated debt upwards of $17,000.

In October of 2008, I was laid off from work along with many other people during the economic downturn.

Jeff and I were married in June of 2012 and together we paid off my car loan of about $5,000.

We prayed about the rest of my debt and felt led to stop using credit cards. We believed that God would pay off our credit card debt if we stopped using them.

Thank God for His super abounding grace. His grace is greater than our mistakes. When money came, Jeff asked God what the money was for, and God said it was to pay off the debt!

That was in October of 2013.

Jeff encouraged me to call each creditor and ask them for the least amount they would require if I was able to pay them in full immediately.

So, I did that. I called each creditor, and God made a way in every situation. I was making payments of $50.00 a month to an attorney. My balance was still $1,900.00, but he shaved off $500 and settled for a lump payment of $1,400.00. He was paid in full that day.

I owed another person $700. She settled for $500.

The next person, to whom I owed $3,200, forgave the full amount in exchange for me relinquishing my percentage of ownership on her house.

I had a student loan that was $3,700. I called to settle accounts but they would not lower it one penny. Nevertheless, it was okay because the savings off of the other debts covered the payoff on the student loan. The process was full of God's fingerprints!

Our good God did something for me which, in my own efforts, would have taken years to accomplish. Debt is a ball-and-chain. It is a trap that I pray the body of Christ would stop falling into.

Proverbs 22:7 says that the borrower is servant to the lender. When I was in debt, I was stressed. It robbed me of my peace and of my health. Now that I have been debt-free for five years, the daily peace I enjoy is priceless. If you are in debt, stop digging. Pray to God and He will deliver you and set you free.

Abundant Grace

Jeff said to me one evening, "From now on we are going to treat Mckayla with nothing but grace and love."

My daughter was eighteen and had been deeply hurt by the church, so she was no longer attending. I had to make an adjustment on the inside.

I was highly criticized growing up, and my tendency was to treat my children with the same harshness that I was shown.

I made the decision to feed on God's grace, which is my daily bread. Naturally, what I was eating I also fed to my children.

I began to pray blessing and encouragement over her. I spoke the blessing of Numbers 6:24-26 over her,

"The Lord bless you and keep you! The Lord make His face to shine upon you and be gracious to you. The Lord lift up His countenance upon you and give you peace. You are my beloved daughter in whom I am well pleased!"

Her face beamed. It was as if life substance reached and filled her. Criticism kills, but grace gives life.

Mckayla had started college and was driving to the other side of town in an old, not so reliable pickup truck. She was in need of a laptop, so we bought her one. Grace repeatedly came through for her. I stopped telling her what she needed to do and started telling her what had been done for her.

After about six months of this, she walked into our home with a smile and hugged me.

This was new!

It was the change we'd been dreaming of, and it was worth every moment of patience, prayer, and transforming my own disposition towards her.

Since I had quit my bus driving job and no longer needed my car so much, Jeff and I decided to give it to Mckayla. Oh, the priceless expression on her face. She later graduated from college with a degree in photography.

My brother is a mechanic and had been without a car for four years. We were able to give him the truck Mckayla was driving, and he was equally blessed.

God's grace has set me free and has allowed me to set others free. The goodness of God knows no limits.

SUPERNATURAL INCREASE

CHAPTER 7

A Blessed Marriage Brings Much Increase

I am constantly praying over Patti that God would give her the desires of her heart. I also proclaim the promises found in this scripture over her:

> **NUMBERS 6:22-27**
> *And the Lord spoke to Moses, saying:*
>
> *"Speak to Aaron and his sons, saying, 'This is the way you shall bless the children of Israel. Say to them:*
>
> *The Lord bless you…"*
>
> ~ Prosperity (3 John 2)

"...and keep you..."

~ Protection (Ps 91)

"...The Lord make His face shine upon you...

~ Presence (Ps 16:11)

"...And be gracious to you..."

~ Provision (Phil 4:19)

"...The Lord lift up His countenance upon you..."

~ Pleasure (Ps 16:11)

"...And give you peace..."

~ Peace (Isa 26:3)

"...So, they shall put my name on the children of Israel, and I will bless them."

Don't Say Things You Will Regret

EPHESIANS 4:29
"Let no corrupt word proceed out of your mouth, but what is good for necessary edification, that it may impart grace to the hearers."

Whatever you sow into your wife will come back to you. If you criticize her, she will criticize you. If you love her, she will love you. I speak words of love over my wife.

I remind her that she is beautiful, sexy, elegant, wonderful, loving, kind, giving and, most of all, godly. I thank her for giving me the greatest gift, which is her love, and which has taught me how to love. I tell her she is a gift from God, His very best for me. When she does things for me, I speak and show my gratitude.

We share everything. We do Bible study together and I get to teach her what God is saying to us as a couple. We regularly discuss what we hear God saying. We have no secrets between us. If I'm struggling with something, I tell her, and she ministers and prays for me. I also do the same for her. The lifetime fruit of a happy, healthy marriage could never be measured.

The Prayer of Agreement

Before we married, Patti, Patti's mother and I prayed for God to give us a house. Patti's mom was eighty-seven years old at the time, and we were praying that God would give us a home near her so that we could always be close by.

The Lord owns the universe. We did not ask for a house to rent or mortgage. We asked Him for a house and stood on His promise for it.

> **MATTHEW 18:19 :**
> *"Again, I say to you that if two of you agree
> on earth concerning anything, it will be done
> for you by my Father in heaven."*

For two months, we prayed for this house, never asking anyone for help.

Then, I got the phone call.

"Do you have a house yet?"

The answer was a resounding no.

He replied, "You pick the house and I will buy it for you."

God was answering our prayer! Not only did we find exactly the house we wanted, it was given to us; and it was right next door to Patti's mom.

Favor of the Lord to Buy A House

ROMANS 8:31 :
What then shall we say to these things? If God is for us, who can be against us?"

"I could lose my license for telling you this," the realtor started, "but I believe you are supposed to have this home."

The house already had thirteen offers, and before all was said and done, there were a total sixteen offers in addition to ours; but the realtor gave us what we needed so we could make the highest offer and win the bidding war.

The first year of taxes were paid and the house was put in my name. That alone was mind-blowing, but we still had no refrigerator, couch, washer or dryer. So, what do you think we did? Did we say, "God has done enough. We can't possibly ask for more"?

Of course not! We asked God for furniture.

In one week, we got another phone call.

"Do you you have any furniture yet?" they asked.

"No," I answered, and the call ended shortly after that.

I assumed they were going to pray for us that God would provide. Never did we look to other people for our provision. We just trusted and waited on our Father.

Another week went by after that call, and we received a letter in the mail with a check for $5,000.00. On the check was a sticky note that said, "Go buy furniture."

At one time, I'd lost everything—house, family, business and even friends and church. I knew I wasn't perfect. I knew I couldn't earn God's blessing. All I could do was trust in Jesus to fulfill His promises of healing and restoration, not because of what I do or how well I do it, but because I am a son.

If I had tried to accomplish all of this on my own, I would have failed. The only obligation of a son or daughter to receive their inheritance is to trust the Father who gives it, and then receive it when it arrives.

Born Again, Born Again Experience

Many years ago, while at a Peggy Cole meeting, she called me out of the crowd and told me to stand up.

"You will have a born again, born again experience!" she prophesied.

I know what that means now. I was given a new life and a new start, with God's grace, love and His mercy.

In a short time, I have a wife who loves me along with 3 kids, a house paid for and put in my name, the yearly taxes paid for, and a house full of furniture.

Shifting into Blessings

While Patti was working as a bus driver, I had a season of much uninterrupted alone-time with God.

"Just because you are spending time with me," He told me one morning, " you are debt-free."

Money began flowing into our lives. A home came. Money to buy furniture for the home followed. Then, more money came in the mail as a confirmation that He was calling me into full-time ministry. On 12/12/12, we received $10,000.

Where God guides, He provides. Heaven is not broke!

I had been set free! I was also praying about Patti being able to quit her job, because I believed we were both called to full-time ministry. As you read earlier, Patti was indeed released from her job. Patti believed that God keeps His Word. She had prayed to retire at a certain age and she did. God keeps His promises.

One-Thousand-Fold Return

We went to see our dear friend Dr. Gershom preach at Breath of His Spirit Church in the LA area. Just before it was over, Dr. Gershom prophesied:

"Whoever gives into tonight's offering will receive a one-thousand times return." Deuteronomy 1:11

Patti looked at me, I looked at her, and we both asked the Lord.

"A hundred dollars," we agreed. We'd heard the same number.

Months went by and nothing came. We waited longer still, and still nothing. So we prayed together and declared that His Word is coming.

If you believe in the Prophets, you will be blessed.

Five months later, on an ordinary day just like any other, it happened. The envelope probably weighed less than one ounce, but inside was a $100,000 check. To say we were undone would be history's greatest understatement. A moment's obedience had become more than most Americans earn in a year's wages. We called our friend and told him how true that word he spoke came to pass.

The next chance we had, we attended Breath of His Spirit Church to hear Dr. Gershom preach, and at the end of his preaching he asked me to share our testimony.

Again, he prophesied the one-thousand-times blessing return on the offering. Again, we both agreed $100 and gave it. This time, it was seven months later we received $100,000. Now, at the writing of this book we own four homes, three of them income-producing, and are debt-free.

MARK 11:24
"Therefore, I say to you, whatever things you ask when you pray, believe that you receive them, and you will have them."

For one of the four homes, I specified to God that I wanted to pay $60,000 for a house with 1,200 square feet, three bedrooms and two bathrooms.

For six months, I strived to no avail. Frustrated and discouraged, I asked God why I was not finding a house. He replied that anything which is frustrating me and causing unfruitfulness is on me, not Him.

"Ok, Lord, so what do you want me to do?"

"Stop trying."

I stopped looking and stopped worrying about finding the house.

One week later, I received an email from my realtor. My Real Estate man found a 1,200 square foot home with three beds and two baths.

I knew this was the house.

"I'll offer $60,000."

The realtor advised me to offer more.

Before I could respond, the Lord spoke to me:

"What price did you ask Me for?"

"$60,000."

Silence.

So, I stood my ground.

"$60,000 is my final offer."

A little while later, my realtor called me—astonished. The owner had accepted my offer.

For the next two months I worked on that house, making it ready to rent. Even then, Patti and I continued to cast our care on the Lord as we asked Him to provide all that was needed to bring the house in order.

God came through.

We needed about $4,000 in electrical work done, but because of God's favor, the electrician offered to do the work for just the price of the wiring.

We also weren't interested in owning an *empty* rental property, so we prayed for the right renter to come quickly.

Almost immediately, a family arrived ready to rent. With joyful faces they told us, "The Lord led us to this home. We knew this was the house."

He answered prayer after prayer. He always has, and He always will. You can never exhaust the goodness or the abundance of God.

CHAPTER 8

The Grace Revolution

Patti and I were introduced to Joseph Prince's Ministry during this time. Prince calls his ministry "The Grace Revolution." His teaching changed our lives.

According to Prince, there are two completely different covenants that Christians have been mixing. Jesus came to *fulfill* the old covenant of law to usher in the new covenant of grace. What a revelation!

We Had Mixture

The mixture Prince warns against is that of the two covenants. Jesus addressed this with the disciples in the Gospel of Luke:

> LUKE 5:36-39
> *"Then He spoke a parable to them: 'No one puts a piece from a new garment on an old*

> *one; otherwise the new makes a tear, and also*
> *the piece that was taken out of the new does*
> *not match the old. And no one puts new wine*
> *into old wineskins; or else the new wine will*
> *burst the wineskins and be spilled, and the*
> *wineskins will be ruined. But new wine must*
> *be put into new wineskins, and both are*
> *preserved. And no one, having drunk*
> *old wine, immediately desires new; for he*
> *says, 'The old is better.'"*

We must always read the Bible through the lens of the cross. Through the cross and because of Jesus, we have been given a new Covenant, a new way we relate to God. For instance:

PSALM 7:11
> *"God is a just Judge who is angry with the*
> *wicked every day."*

Is that true today, or did God do something that changes everything? What do you do with this scripture?

This scripture PS 7:11 does not apply today.

2 TIMOTHY 2:15
> *"Be diligent to present yourself approved to*
> *God, a worker who does not need to be*
> *ashamed, rightly dividing the word of truth."*

2 CORINTHIANS 5:19
> *"That is, that God was in Christ reconciling*
> *the world to Himself, not imputing their*
> *trespasses to them, and has committed to us*
> *the word of reconciliation."*

So, is God still angry with the wicked every day? Or did the cross make a difference? Is God still going to judge cities?

If the Father judges cities because of their sin, then He is going to have to apologize to Jesus, because Jesus died for the sins of the world. Which one is it?

The scriptures clearly teaches that Jesus died for our sins so that all of humanity can be right before God (meaning there are only believers and unbelievers). Yet, there are people prophesying that California will be thrown into the sea because of sin.

They don't know what covenant they are speaking from. James and John, the Sons of Thunder, wanted to call down fire on a people who did not welcome the Lord. How did Jesus reply?

> **LUKE 9:54**
> *"And when His disciples James and John saw this, they said, 'Lord, do You want us to command fire to come down from heaven and consume them, just as Elijah did?'*
>
> *But He turned and rebuked them, and said, 'You do not know what manner of spirit you are of. For the Son of Man did not come to destroy men's lives but to save them.' And they went to another village."*

Man could not and cannot save himself; so, Christ did the work on our behalf. All that is left for us to experience His salvation, deliverance and justification is to believe.

Grace Versus Law

The law demands what we could not supply, but Grace supplies all that is required from God.

JOHN 1:17
"For the law was given through Moses, but grace and truth came through Jesus Christ."

HEBREWS 10:1
"For the law, having a shadow of the good things to come..."

JAMES 2:10 (NASB)
"For whoever keeps the whole law and yet stumbles in one point, he has become guilty of all."

TITUS 2:11-12 (NIV)
"For the grace of God has appeared that offers salvation to all people. It teaches us to say 'No' to ungodliness and worldly passions, and to live self-controlled, upright and godly lives in this present age..."

- Jesus was concealed in the Old Testament and revealed in the New Testament.

- The law condemns the best of us, but grace justifies the worst of us.

- No one is justified by keeping the law.

- The old and the new covenant are as different as night and day.

LUKE 18:9-14

"Also, He spoke this parable to some who trusted in themselves that they were righteous, and despised others:

"Two men went up to the temple to pray, one a Pharisee and the other a tax collector. The Pharisee stood and prayed thus with himself, 'God, I thank You that I am not like other men —extortioners, unjust, adulterers, or even as this tax collector. I fast twice a week; I give tithes of all that I possess.'

"And the tax collector, standing afar off, would not so much as raise his eyes to heaven, but beat his breast, saying, 'God, be merciful to me a sinner!'

"I tell you, this man went down to his house justified rather than the other; for everyone who exalts himself will be humbled, and he who humbles himself will be exalted."

In this parable, the Pharisee justified himself by keeping the law. God did not honor the Pharisee but honored the tax collector who asked for God's mercy and grace, being aware that he sinned. God resists the proud and gives grace to the humble.

Controversies Surrounding the Gospel of Grace

Why is there so much controversy surrounding the Gospel of Grace?

The enemy is aware that the moment you learn to receive God's grace, you will begin to reign in life. Because he knows this, he sends obstacles and builds fences to shut people out from the Gospel of Grace. Patti and I started to Reign under the Gospel of Grace.

YOU WERE MADE TO REIGN IN LIFE!

ROMANS 5:17
"For if by the one man's offense death reigned through the one, much more those who receive abundance of grace and of the gift of righteousness will reign in life through the One, Jesus Christ."

REVELATION 5:10
"And have made us kings and priests to our God; And we shall reign on the earth."

...As Jesus is in this world, so are you.

- The gift of righteousness is a gift freely given to you, once and for all.

- You were made to reign in life.

- You are called a king and a priest.

- Every place you do not Reign, the Devil is.

1 JOHN 4:17
"Love has been perfected among us in this: that we may have boldness in the day of judgment; because as He is, so are we in this world."

LIES About Grace

These are just a few of the most prominent lies concerning grace.

LIE – You can lose your salvation.

Anything that is based in fear is not God. (What I mean by this, God gives us assurance of salvation) Yes, there are some scriptures that seem to suggest that you can lose your salvation, but these scriptures must be read in light of their *context*, and according to the full counsel of the New Testament. There are many more scriptures that make it clear that salvation through Christ is certain:

> ### JOHN 10:27-30
> *"My sheep hear My voice, and I know them, and they follow Me. And I give them eternal life, and they shall never perish; neither shall anyone snatch them out of My hand. My Father, who has given them to Me, is greater than all; and no one is able to snatch them out of My Father's hand. I and My Father are one."*

"I give them eternal life." How long is eternal life?

"They shall never perish." This means they will never be lost.

"Neither shall anyone snatch them out of my hand." Jesus is able to keep us.

"No one is able to snatch them out of my Father's hand."
Wow!

JOHN 3:16
*"For God so loved the world that He gave His
only begotten Son that whoever believes in
Him should not perish but have eternal life."*

He sent Jesus so that anyone who believes will have eternal
life. Eternal life is just that—forever. It cannot come to an
end. The question is never whether God has granted eternal
salvation, but only whether you and I will believe and
therefore walk in it.

LIE – God saved you. Now you have to work out your salvation.

Philippians 2:12 tells us to work out our salvation with fear
and trembling.

Read verse 13:

"For it is God who works in you both to will and do for His
good pleasure."

The apostle Paul said that he worked hard, but it was the
grace of God that empowered him.

1 CORINTHIANS 15:10
*"By the grace of God, I am what I am, and
His grace toward me was not in vain; but I
labored more abundantly than they all, yet not
I, but the grace of God which was with me."*

LIE – We still have to keep the Ten Commandments.

If you put yourself back under the law, you put yourself back under the curse.

GALATIANS 3:10
"For as many as are of the works of the law are under the curse; for it is written, 'Cursed is everyone who does not continue in all things which are written in the book of the law, to do them.'"

1 JOHN 3:22-23
"And whatever we ask we receive from Him, because we keep His commandments and do those things that are pleasing in His sight. And this is His commandment: that we should believe on the name of His Son Jesus Christ and love one another, as He gave us commandment."

COLOSSIANS 3:3
"For you died, and your life is hidden with Christ in God."

GALATIANS 3:24-25
"Therefore, the law was our tutor to bring us to Christ, that we might be justified by faith. But after faith has come, we are no longer under a tutor."

GALATIANS 2:16
"Knowing that a man is not justified by the works of the law but by faith in Jesus Christ,

*even we have believed in Christ Jesus, that we
might be justified by faith in Christ and not by
the works of the law; for by the works of the
law no flesh shall be justified."*

MATTHEW 5:17
*"Do not think that I came to destroy the Law
or the Prophets. I did not come to destroy but
to fulfill."*

HEBREWS 8:13
*"In that He says, 'A new covenant,' He has
made the first obsolete. Now what is becoming
obsolete and growing old is ready to vanish
away."*

Read Romans 7:1-6. This passage clearly teaches that you
have been legally unbound from the law by the death of
Christ.

ROMANS 7:4
*"Therefore, my brethren, you also have
become dead to the law through the body of
Christ, that you may be married to another—
to Him who was raised from the dead, that we
should bear fruit to God."*

This is why Jesus died for you. He died to free you from the
first marriage to The Law, that you could enter into a new
covenant with a new Bridegroom—Himself—Jesus.

ROMANS 7:4 (TPT)
*"So, my dear brothers and sisters, the same
principle applies to your relationship with
God. For you died to your first husband, the
law, by being co-crucified with the body of the*

Messiah. So you are now free to "marry" another—the one who was raised from the dead so that you may now bear spiritual fruit for God."

LIE – When you preach grace, you give people a license to sin.

First of all, this is a misunderstanding of grace. In His mercy, God forgives us of our sin. Grace, however, is not pardon but power. It is enabling power to live righteously (see Titus 2:11-12).

According to Romans 5:17, the more Grace you receive the more you reign in life.

> *JOHN 8:10-11*
> *"He said to her, 'Woman, where are those accusers of yours? Has no one condemned you?'*
>
> *She said, 'No one, Lord.'*
>
> *And Jesus said to her, 'Neither do I condemn you; go and sin no more.'"*

The woman caught in adultery sinned but received no condemnation from Jesus. Instead, in His command to "sin no more," I believe He imparted to her the grace to walk free from sin, just as He has done for you and me.

> **3 JOHN 1:4 (NIV)**
> *"I have no greater joy than to hear that my children are walking in the truth."*

Renew your mind to the truth.
Right thinking = right believing = right living.

> **ROMANS 12:1-2 (ESV)**
> *"I appeal to you therefore, brothers, by the
> mercies of God, to present your bodies as a
> living sacrifice, holy and acceptable to God,
> which is your spiritual worship. Do not be
> conformed to this world, but be transformed
> by the renewal of your mind, that by testing
> you may discern what is the will of God, what
> is good and acceptable and perfect."*

To be under grace is to have victory over sin.

> **ROMANS 6:14**
> *"For sin shall not have dominion over you,
> for you are not under law but under grace."*

LIE – If you preach grace, it will bring a sin revival.

The truth is that if you preach the law, you will bring a sin
revival.

> **1 CORINTHIANS 15:56**
> *"The sting of death is sin, and the strength of
> sin is the law."*

Preaching religious rules and regulations strengthens the
power of sin in us; but grace empowers us to love God and
walk with Him.

CHAPTER 9

Supernatural Increase Manual

PART I: FOUNDATIONS OF GRACE

In order to experience the blessing, Patti and I had to change our minds and believe that God really wants to bless us. We had to shift from relying on our own striving and self-efforts to believing in God's grace to fulfill all His promises and the desires of our hearts.

At one time, we thought we had to "do it all," but hearing the Gospel of Grace deepened our faith that God is really good and He wants to bring us nothing but blessings.

> **JOHN 6:28-29 (NIV)**
> *"Then they asked Him, 'What must we do to do the works God requires?"*

Jesus answered, 'The work of God is this: to believe in the one He has sent.'"

This is what God wants from us: to trust Him.

What do we believe about prosperity? Is God a rich Dad or a poor Dad?

LIE – God wants us poor to keep us humble.

What earthly father wants his children poor and struggling? If you are a mother or a father, don't you want the best for your children?

2 CORINTHIAN 8:9
"For you know the grace of our Lord Jesus Christ, that though He was rich, yet for your sake He became poor, that you through His poverty might become rich."

3 JOHN 2
"Beloved, I pray that you may prosper in all things and be in health, just as your soul prospers."

LIE – If God gave us wealth, it would corrupt us.

We have been given a new heart and a new Spirit from God. We have been given God's heart and His dreams.

God comes alongside of us and teaches us so we have the right motives.

1 JOHN 2:27
"But the anointing which you have received from Him abides in you, and you do not need that anyone teach you; but as the same anointing teaches you concerning all things, and is true, and is not a lie, and just as it has taught you, you will abide in Him."

EPHESIANS 3:20
"Now to Him who is able to do exceedingly abundantly above all that we ask or think, according to the power that works in us."

LIE – Wealth is of the world and we are not to be of the world.

PROVERBS 3:9 (NLT)
"Honor the LORD with your wealth and with the best part of everything you produce."

It was God who anointed David as king and gave him great wealth, and God who gives you the ability to create wealth. God's heart towards David is that God would have done much more.

2 SAMUEL 12:8 (NLT)
"I gave you your master's house and his wives and the kingdoms of Israel and Judah. And if that had not been enough, I would have given you much, much more."

DEUTERONOMY 8:18 (NIV)
"But remember the LORD your God, for it is He who gives you the ability to produce wealth, and so confirms His covenant, which He swore to your ancestors, as it is today."

You need supplies so you can fulfill your calling and complete your mission on earth.

PHILIPPINES 4:19
"...and my God shall supply all your needs according to His riches in glory by Christ Jesus."

PSALM 1:1-3
"Blessed is the man who walks not in the counsel of the ungodly, nor stands in the path of sinners, nor sits in the seat of the scornful; But his delight is in the law of the Lord, and in His law, he meditates day and night. He shall be like a tree planted by the rivers of water that brings forth its fruit in its season, whose leaf also shall not wither; and whatever he does shall prosper."

The Gospel of Jesus Christ leads to blessing, success, healing, restoration, protection, financial breakthrough, security, peace, wholeness, reconciliation and much, much more.

Remember: it is the Gospel that seems too good to be true. "Gospel" is translated *Good News* for a reason. It may sound too good to be true, but it is not! It is exactly good, and it is exactly true.

Man's Greatest Failure is Not Believing in the Goodness of God

(1) God brought Israel out of Egypt to "a land flowing with milk and honey"; yet, they never went into the land. Forty years later, a new generation entered the promise. Their fathers failed because they did not have faith. They simply did not believe in the goodness of God to bring them through the obstacles in fulfillment of His own promise.

(2) God said in Deuteronomy 6:11, "I had houses for you that you did not build, and I had vineyards for you that you did not plant" (and much more). Again, they failed to believe it and, therefore, failed to receive it.

(3) If you don't believe God is good, you will have a hard time receiving from Him. You may accept hardship as from Him when it is not and refuse to receive the greater blessings that truly come from His hand simply because you don't expect God to be that good.

(4) If you don't receive from God, you will not be blessed; but James 1:17 says, "Every good and perfect gift is from above, coming down from the Father of the heavenly lights, who does not change like shifting shadows."

New Wineskin

For us to believe how good God is, we must get rid of our old wine skins.

Jesus said to beware of the leaven of the Pharisees.

The leaven of Pharisees is self-righteousness, hypocrisy and self-effort.

The Pharisees justified themselves by keeping the law. Yet, the scripture is explicit that no one can keep the law and be right before God. If some could, then some could also boast and bring glory to themselves. Our righteousness is not to bring ourselves glory, but to glorify God.

> **GALATIANS 2:16 (NIV)**
> *"...know that a person is not justified by the works of the law, but by faith in Jesus Christ. So we, too, have put our faith in Christ Jesus that we may be justified by faith in Christ and not by the works of the law, because by the works of the law no one will be justified."*

No more do, do, doo-doo! It has been done! You are complete in Him. When Jesus was on the cross, He said, "It Is Finished."

> **EPHESIANS 2:8-9**
> *"For by grace you have been saved through faith, and that not of yourselves; it is the gift of God, not of works, lest anyone should boast."*

Faith gives you the eyes to see the truth that Jesus already died for your sins two-thousand years ago.

Leaven in Christianity

The leaven in Christianity is the mixing of the two covenants. It is rooted in self-effort and failing to give God all the glory by putting our confidence in what we can do.

Where were you when Christ died for you? Was it your plan to get saved? The Bible says you did not love Him except that He loved you first.

You did not choose Him first. He chose you.

No one comes to Christ unless the Father draws him.

So, who gets the glory for salvation?

Our work in salvation is to lay down our efforts and simply accept what He has already done.

> **EPHESIANS 2:1-2, 4-5 (NASB)**
> *"And you were dead in your trespasses and sins, in which you formerly walked according to the course of this world... But God, being rich in mercy, because of His great love with which He loved us, even when we were dead in our transgressions, made us alive together with Christ (by grace you have been saved)."*

Can a dead person save himself? While you were dead in sins and trespasses, Christ saved you and gave you eternal life.

Or where were you two-thousand years ago? When Jesus went to the cross for you, did He talk it over with you first?

Taking your sin onto Himself and redeeming you forever actually had nothing to do with you. It was *His* decision.

He did not just die for you. He died *as* you.

Again, "...it is the gift of God, not of works, lest anyone should boast."

So, lay down your efforts and give Him all the glory.

Paul's Example of the Gospel of Grace

ROMANS 2:16
"In that day, God will judge the secrets of men by Jesus Christ according to my Gospel."

How did Paul get saved? Where was the altar-call?

GALATIANS 1:1
"Paul, an apostle (not from men nor through man, but through Jesus Christ and God the Father who raised Him from the dead)."

God chose Paul and called him to write thirteen books of the New Testament. He was not one of the twelve with Jesus. Paul had such insight on grace he even corrected Peter, one of the "12 apostles," as we see in Galatians 2.

Repent of self-righteousness and self-effort to give God all the glory.

Sometimes, when we have walked with the Lord for a long time, we forget how broken we were when we first met Him. We color it up. We lose sight of our hopelessness to live right with God without our Savior.

God said to me, "Son, I am *the* Savior. No one else can save. This is my grace."

Don't brag about loving God. Be like John who bragged about how much God loved him.

You will stumble in pride if you brag about how much you love God. There is no comparison to how much God loves you! It's not even close.

We are to remind ourselves daily that we have been forgiven of all our sins.

> **2 PETER 1:5-10**
> *"But also for this very reason, giving all diligence, add to your faith virtue, to virtue knowledge, to knowledge self-control, to self-control perseverance, to perseverance godliness, to godliness brotherly kindness, and to brotherly kindness love. For if these things are yours and abound, you will be neither barren nor unfruitful in the knowledge of our Lord Jesus Christ. For he who lacks these things is shortsighted, even to blindness, and has forgotten that he was cleansed from his old sins."*

Don't forget of how much you have been forgiven.

Verse 10 says we will never stumble:

> *"Therefore, brethren, be even more diligent to make your call and election sure, for if you do these things you will never stumble."*

It is time for you to make a stand by faith in what God says in His Word."Do not waiver in your faith. Believe that God will come through, no matter what."

Eight Steps to Walk in Supernatural Increase

1. Do Not Worry

PHILIPPIANS 4:19
And my God shall supply all your need according to His riches in glory by Christ Jesus.

God's Word to my wife and I was that I was no longer in construction, and we were both in full-time ministry. We were following God and listening to Him. Neither of us had paid work.

We watched as our bank account dropped down to $27; but we were never late on even one bill. We did not try to make things happen to bring in money. God brought money at the right time so that we paid our bills in-full, and on time. God kept His Word. Choose His Word above your circumstances.

MATTHEW 6:33
"First seek the Kingdom of God and righteousness and all these things will be added to you."

We followed Him and He added to us. God will always meet your needs and your wants. He does this through relationship.

PSALM 37:4
*"Delight yourself also in the Lord, and He
shall give you the desires of your heart."*

Believe beyond basic needs. As you enjoy God and give
your life to trusting Him, you can believe beyond survival to
dreams and delights.

MATTHEW 6:25-26 & 33
*"Therefore, I say to you, do not worry about
your life, what you will eat, or what you will
drink; nor about your body, what you will put
on. Is not life more than food and the body
more than clothing? Look at the birds of the
air, for they neither sow nor reap nor gather
into barns; yet your heavenly Father feeds
them. Are you not of more value than they?
You are more valuable than Birds but, seek
first the kingdom of God and His
righteousness, and all these things shall be
added to you."*

You are the Righteous of God and all things shall be added
to you. This is a job offer. Will you take the job? The pay is
everything will be added to you.

GENESIS 3:17 (THE CURSE OF MAN)
*"Then to Adam God said, because you heeded
the voice of your wife, and have eaten of the
tree, of which I commanded you, saying, You,
shall not eat of it: cursed is the ground for
your sake; in toil you shall eat of it all the
days of your life."*

Toil is sorrow, pain, labor and hardship. Worry is rooted in
fear.

God took care of Adam in the beginning. Then, Adam and Eve became like rebellious teenagers who were kicked out of the house. The curse of man is having to fend for himself, but you have been redeemed from the curse!

Faith breaks the power of the curse in your life. Trust God and believe in what Jesus did on the cross for you. He broke all the curses. I'll say it again: the curse is broken!

> **GALATIANS 3:13-14**
> *"Christ has redeemed us from the curse of the law, having become a curse for us for it is written, 'Cursed is everyone who hangs on a tree,' that the blessing of Abraham might come upon the Gentiles in Christ Jesus, that we might receive the promise of the Spirit through faith."*

When Christ was in the Garden of Gethsemane He was literally sweating drops of blood. These blood drops hit the ground and broke the curse off the ground.

Jesus was in anguish for you so that you would not have to be in anguish. Let there be no more worry, fear or anxiety over you. Come out of agreement with it because it is not your portion.

The curse is human effort instead of God's grace. Now, let God take care of you and give you peace. Trusting in what Christ did for you breaks the curse.

This prayer is for anyone who feels unfruitful and wants to become fruitful.

PRAY THIS:

"I stop self-effort in my life. Now, I make a shift to trust in Jesus, His grace and His Word. I believe that God can meet my needs and the desires of my heart. I am more valuable than the birds and I am made in the image of God."

Your Needs

> **PHILIPPIANS 4:19**
> *"And my God shall supply all your need according to His riches in glory by Christ Jesus."*

Your Desires

> **PSALM 37:4**
> *"Delight yourself also in the Lord, and He shall give you the desires of your heart."*

Your Value

> **MATTHEW 6:25-26**
> *"Look at the birds of the air, for they neither sow nor reap nor gather into barns; yet your heavenly Father feeds them. Are you not of more value than they?"*

Your Job

> **MATTHEW 6:33**
> *"But seek first the kingdom of God and His righteousness, and all these things shall be added to you."*

Your Identity

> **GENESIS 1:26-27**
> *"Then God said, 'Let Us make man in Our image, according to Our likeness.'"*

The Woman's Curse

> **GENESIS 3:16**
> *"I will greatly multiply your sorrow and your conception; In pain you shall bring forth children; Your desire shall be for your husband, and he shall rule over you."*

The Man's Curse

> **GENESIS 3:17**
> *"Cursed is the ground for your sake; in toil you shall eat of it all the days of your life."*

All the curses have been broken

> **GALATIANS 3:13**
> *"Christ has redeemed us from the curse of the law."*

Your Blessing

> **GALATIANS 3:14**
> *"...that the blessing of Abraham might come upon the Gentiles in Christ Jesus, that we might receive the promise of the Spirit through faith."*

2. Honor God

Giving is honoring God in our finances. Patti and I gave every time we went to a conference or church. We did not have much. We gave one dollar. We gave fifty-cents. Later, when more money came, we gave much more.

You cannot out-give God.

Try it. You may find yourself making a living on giving! The more you give, the more it comes back to you.

The world's kingdom is upside-down from God's. In the world, people try to get all they can get; but the Kingdom operates not out of getting but giving. The more you give away, the more it returns to you. Then, you become a resource to others rather than looking to others for resource.

Honoring God with your money demonstrates your gratitude and trust.

Honor God and give to the work of the Lord. Give at least 10%. This shows that you trust the Lord and believe His Word.

> **PROVERBS 3:9-10**
> *"Honor the Lord with your possessions."*

Use them for the Kingdom.

> *"…and with the first fruits of all your increase;"*

Give your best offering- as God did in Jesus.

> *"…so your barns will be filled with plenty,"*

You'll have more than enough.

"...and your vats will overflow with new wine."

Holy Spirit will flow in your life.

Be a pipeline, which supplies for yourself and others. Don't be a plate. Being a plate means "The buck stops here," or "It is just for me."

Why Should We Give?

A. Give so you can help others. God does not need the money!
B. Give to keep your heart from greed.
C. Give in demonstration of your trust in God.
D. Give to break the spirit of poverty.

Your supply will come to you because you help others.

The Spirit of Poverty

The spirit of poverty isn't necessarily about being poor. It is about fear; fear that if you give, you will end up poor. That is what keeps you poor!

This is the wrong mentality. Quit saying you don't have enough. Trust me, it is not the Holy Spirit inspiring those words.

If lack is your experience, perhaps it is because you keep speaking lack over your life. You will have what you say.

God is rich. He is your Dad. He loves you.

My wife and I say, "God is buying."

We also say, "We are rich!"

We say that now, and we said it when we had little-to-no money in the bank.

It is More Blessed to Give

My friend came to me in church one Sunday and complained that he didn't have enough money to pay his bills. He said he had $20 to his name.

I told him to give the $20 to God in the offering that morning.

He was shocked, but he rose to the challenge.

As he was headed back to his seat from giving in the offering, a man came over and handed him a check for $300.

Do you believe that you can out-give God? Go ahead. Give it a try! It'll never happen.

Sowing & Reaping

2 CORINTHIANS 9:6
"But this I say; he who sows sparingly will also reap sparingly, and he who sows bountifully will also reap bountifully."

Joy in Giving

> **2 CORINTHIANS 9:7**
> *"So, let each one give as he purposes in his heart, not grudgingly or of necessity; for God loves a cheerful giver."*

The most fulfilled life is the life of one who helps others, and who gives.

CHALLENGE!

Give an offering to a great need in the body. This will break the spirit of poverty. Give to widows, orphans, single moms and anyone who is hurting. When you see your money blessing people, it blesses you. Help the poor and give to the poor. If you give to the poor, you give to the Lord.

3. Be Accountable

If you have debt, it is time to settle all your accounts. Create a document or write down all that you owe in one total amount.

List every monthly expense.

Then, note all your current income.

If your monthly expenses are more than your income, cut out anything unnecessary.

Especially if you already have debt, cut up your credit cards. Stop using them altogether.

Step up to the debt; meaning, FACE IT. Take responsibility.

Call your creditors and offer to pay them in a lump sum or work out a payment schedule. Many will reduce or even forgive your debt just because you called and made the offer.

With all your expenses and financial obligations listed on one page, ask God for wisdom.

If you need more monthly income, ask God for it.

Patti and I do our books and pay our bills once every week. Sometimes, we pay bills before they are due. It feels good to honor your financial obligations and stay "in the black."

On Credit Cards

Patti and I had to repent from relying on credit when we should have relied on God.

We decided that we would only use credit cards for two things: online purchases and hotel reservations.

Consider the literal definition of credit:

1. commendation or honor given for some action, quality, etc. Give credit where it is due.

2. a source of pride or honor
   (from www.dictionary.com)

"Credit" means to give praise (commendation) or honor.

When you borrow from the world, you give praise and honor to the world.

If you refuse to give in to fear, you will see that God comes through every time, and you will bring Him praise, honor and glory.

Why borrow? I have never seen God's answer to a prayer come through the chains of borrowing. Heaven is not broke. We all have a direct line to God—through prayer!

Wherever God Guides, He Provides

Do you have an unmet need? Are you doing God's will?

Here is a simple tip: if you cannot afford it, then do not buy it. This is one way God will lead you. If He hasn't given you the money for it, it is not time to buy it. God's will is God's bill and *God pays all His bills*.

> **ROMANS 13:8**
> *"Owe no one anything except to love one another, for he who loves another has fulfilled the law. You owe people your love."*

> **PSALM 37:21**
> *"The wicked borrowed and don't pay back: but the righteous is merciful and gives. (We are not the wicked.)*

> **DEUTERONOMY 28:12**
> *"You shall loan and not borrow."*

> **EPHESIANS 4:28**
> *"Let him who stole steal no longer, but rather let him labor, working with his hands what is*

good, that he may have something to give him who has need."

Christ paid for your debt on the cross.

COLOSSIANS 2:14
"Having wiped out the handwriting of requirements that was against us, which was contrary to us. And He has taken it out of the way, having nailed it to the cross."

If you get behind on credit cards, even one month, stop using them.

When you step up to pay your debt, God will put money in your hand. Why? Because He honors His Word.

PROVERBS 22:7
"...a borrower is a slave to the lender."

If you are in debt, you are a slave. And Jesus came to set the slaves free!

Don't let debt come back.

GALATIANS 5:1
"Stand fast therefore in the liberty by which Christ has made us free, and do not be entangled again with a yoke of bondage."

In Summary:

1. Know your monthly expenses. What does it cost to meet life's basic needs each month?
2. Know your monthly income.

3. Do not spend more than your income.
4. Cut the fat. Get rid of things you don't need.
5. Only buy what you can afford.
6. Ask God for what you need.

PRAY THIS:

I repent for trusting in credit cards or loans. Now, I put my trust in You, God, and You alone, especially in the area of my finances."

You may be inclined to cut up your credit cards. Ask God to make you debt-free. Step up to all that you owe and thank God in advance for the money.

4. Stewardship

In 1996, God told me that He was making me a steward over His finances. I did not yet know what that meant, but He continued to teach me many more things about finances. He put impressions on my heart, causing me to know what to do and where to plant financial seeds at just the right time.

It is time for you to give God everything you own.

Patti and I brought everything we owned and dedicated it all to God. It's His anyway, but we wanted to come into full agreement with the truth.

We declared that He owns it, and it all belongs to Him to use as He pleases.

If God tells us to put money in an offering, we will put money in an offering. If He tells us to give a house away, we will give a house away.

At different times, when God gave us money, I would ask God where to give the tithe. Most often, it was the church; but other times, He had us give to people that were in need.

I may not have known of their need at the time, but God knew.

When you give God everything, He will speak to you and give you guidance. Ask God each time that you receive money with the simple question, "What is this money for?" He will tell you.

Stewardship is taking care of someone else's goods. Everything you own belongs to God. So, when you steward well, you are taking good care of God's goods.

> **1 CORINTHIANS 4:2**
> *"Moreover, it is required in stewards that one is found faithful."*

> **LUKE 16:11**
> *"Therefore if you have not been faithful in the unrighteous mammon, who will commit to your trust the true riches? "*

> **LUKE 16:12**
> *"And if you have not been faithful in what is another man's, who will give you what is your own?"*

The Parable of the Talents

MATTHEW 25:14-30

"For the kingdom of heaven is like a man traveling to a far country, who called his own servants and delivered his goods to them. And to one he gave five talents, to another two, and to another one, to each according to his own ability; and immediately he went on a journey. Then he who had received the five talents went and traded with them, and made another five talents. And likewise, he who had received two gained two more also. But he who had received one went and dug in the ground, and hid his lord's money. After a long time, the lord of those servants came and settled accounts with them. So, he who had received five talents came and brought five other talents, saying, 'Lord, you delivered to me five talents; look, I have gained five more talents besides them.' His lord said to him, 'Well done, good and faithful servant; you were faithful over a few things, I will make you ruler over many things. Enter into the joy of your lord.' He also who had received two talents came and said, 'Lord, you delivered to me two talents; look, I have gained two more talents besides them.' His lord said to him, 'Well done, good and faithful servant; you have been faithful over a few things, I will make you ruler over many things. Enter into the joy of your lord.' Then he who had received the one talent came and said, 'Lord, I knew you to be a hard man..." (He did not know the Lord to be Good.) *"...reaping*

113

*where you have not sown, and gathering
where you have not scattered seed. And I was
afraid, and went and hid your talent in the
ground. Look, there you have what is yours.'
But his lord answered and said to him, 'You
wicked and lazy servant, you knew that I reap
where I have not sown, and gather where I
have not scattered seed. So you ought to have
deposited my money with the bankers, and at
my coming I would have received back my
own with interest. Therefore, take the talent
from him, and give it to him who has ten
talents. 'For to everyone who has, more will
be given, and he will have abundance; but
from him who does not have, even what he has
will be taken away. And cast the unprofitable
servant into the outer darkness. There will be
weeping and gnashing of teeth.'" (emphasis
added)*

If this is a weakness in your life, study the scriptures
concerning stewardship and let His Word renew your mind
so you can overcome!

PRAY THIS:

*Father, I recognize that everything I own belongs to You, and
I dedicate it back to You. Make me an excellent steward over
money and the resources You've given me. Thank You for
Your constant guidance.*

Your dedication gives God permission to be Lord over your
resources and to instruct you!

5. True Wealth Comes from God

God gives us wisdom and blesses us to produce wealth.

Years ago, within two weeks of work in my construction company, I had made $100,000. I knew it was the Lord's blessing on my life, because He not only showed me how to secure the finances but He taught me how to be a better builder and gave me wisdom to do great work in construction!

The only requirement to have this experience is to enjoy relationship with God. Because you know Him, you may freely ask of Him what you want. True wealth is and comes through your relationship with Him.

> DEUTERONOMY 8:18
> *"And you shall remember the Lord your God,*
> *for it is He who gives you power to get wealth*
> *that He may establish His covenant which He*
> *swore to your fathers, as it is this day."*

Prosperity comes from meditation on God's Word.

> PSALM 1:1-3
> *"Blessed is the man…"*
>
> A happy man - God is blessing every area in his life.

"…Who walks not in the counsel of the ungodly,"

Those who don't believe in God.

"…Nor stands in the path of sinners,"

Those who do not stop doing wrong.

"…Nor sits in the seat of the scornful;"

Those who are negative, see the cup half empty.

"…But his delight is in the law of the Lord,"

The law of Grace and Love.

"…And in His law he meditates day and night…"

He thinks about what God's Word says.

"…He shall be like a tree planted by the rivers of water,"

Water is represented by Holy Spirit.

"…That brings forth its fruit in its season,"

Fruit is a blessed life.

"…Whose leaf also shall not wither;"

Always has a supply coming to them.

"…And whatever he does shall prosper."

God answered Solomon's request and much more.

1 Kings 3-9	Solomon asked for wisdom
1 Kings 3:10	The speech pleased the Lord
1 Kings 3:11	Because you have asked this thing
1 Kings 3:12	I have done according to your words
1 Kings 3:13	And extra, both riches and honor

Prosperity comes from knowing God.

God told me, "I am the best investment one could ever have. Because you have spent time with Me, you are debt-free. Men go after gold and silver but I am your investment that will pay off in every way. For I know your heart's desire and I will fulfill it. I delight in blessing you."

PRAY THIS:

God, I ask for a Holy Spirit impartation to create wealth. Make me to know You deeper and delight in You more than ever. Thank You for giving me wisdom and the treasures of heaven.

6. Sowing and Reaping

This chapter is about receiving the blessing Jesus has already accomplished for us. You are receiving all the benefits of the cross and the inheritance in Jesus Christ.

The blessing of prosperity is part of the Gospel of Christ. All of the promises of your inheritance are in His Word.

If someone dies and leaves you an inheritance, you simply need to read it in the will. The Bible is the will of God for your life.

You have heard of sowing and reaping; how about reaping what Jesus sowed on the cross for you?

Will the Lamb receive His full reward?

Everything He accomplished and bought for you on the cross, He wants you to have. If you don't receive what He did for you, you are being ripped off, and so is Jesus!

If you receive all that Jesus died for you to have, you will be blessed.

This is not the "Prosperity Gospel," but a reminder that abundance is part of the Gospel, which promises salvation, healing, restoration, provision, health, joy, peace, and love.

2 CORINTHIANS 8:9
"For you know the grace of our Lord Jesus Christ, that though He was rich, yet for your sakes He became poor, that you through His poverty might become rich."

You get Jesus' inheritance!

PROVERBS 10:22
*"The blessing of the Lord makes one rich and
He adds no sorrow with it."*

ROMANS 8:16-17
*"The Spirit Himself bears witness with our
spirit that we are children of God, and if
children, then heirs—heirs of God and joint
heirs with Christ, if indeed we suffer with
Him, that we may also be glorified together."*

Jesus has access to the Father and so do you. The veil was
torn from top to bottom. God already did the greatest thing
He could do for us.

ROMANS 8:31-32
*"What then shall we say to these things? If
God is for us, who can be against us? He who
did not spare His own Son, but delivered Him
up for us all, how shall He not with Him also
freely give us all things?"*

ROMANS 5:17
*"For if by the one man's offense death reigned
through the one, much more those who receive
abundance of grace and of the gift of
righteousness will reign in life through the
One, Jesus Christ."*

He will give you more than what you ask, so ask bigger.

EPHESIANS 3:20
*"Now to Him who is able to do exceedingly
abundantly above all that we ask or think,
according to the power that works in us."*

PRAY THIS:

I believe that riches are a part of the Gospel and I ask to receive everything Jesus paid for.

7. Thousand-Times Blessing

The thousand-times blessing is mentioned in Deuteronomy 1:11. It is God's heart that you are fruitful and that you multiply and have dominion and fill the earth. I have received a large thousand-times blessing twice. On two separate occasions we gave $100, and later received $100,000!

God's desire is to have a relationship with you and to bless you. God is a great Father. Which good father does not want to bless his kids?

> **DEUTERONOMY 1:11**
> *"May the Lord God of your father's make you a thousand times more numerous than you are, and bless you as He promised."*

The word "thousand" means vindication of wrong done to you. If you have been wronged, then God will vindicate you… a thousand times!

> **GENESIS 20:7**
> *"Now therefore, restore the man's wife; for he is a prophet, and he will pray for you and you shall live. But if you do not restore her, know that you shall surely die you and all who are yours."* (God defending Abraham)

GENESIS 20:16 (NASB)
"To Sarah he said, 'Behold, I have given your brother a thousand pieces of silver; behold, it is your vindication before all who are with you, and before all men you are cleared.'"

First mentioned of "The Blessing" also comes to us by God's promise to Abraham; Read Genesis 12:1-3, *"In you all the nations shall be blessed…"*

GALATIANS 3:7-9
"Therefore know that only those who are of faith are sons of Abraham. And the Scripture, foreseeing that God would justify the Gentiles by faith, preached the gospel to Abraham beforehand, saying, 'In you all the nations shall be blessed.' So then those who are of faith are blessed with believing Abraham."

PRAY THIS:

Father, in any way that I have been wronged, I do not look to man's justice, but ask You to vindicate and restore all that was taken, one-thousand times!

8 Give Testimony of the Goodness of the Lord in the Land of the Living

I have listed things that God did for me. These are part of my testimony. As you hear them, you can say to the Lord in any area you need, "Do them again, Lord, in my life!" Likewise, as you testify to the good works of God, you multiply the blessing in your life and the lives of your hearers.

You may have heard of the fictional character and movie, *Dennis the Menace*.

In one scene, Dennis exclaimed (my paraphrase), "Let's go over to Mrs. Wilson's house and get some cookies!"

His friend reminded Dennis that he is always doing something bad to them, wondering why he thought they would want to give him, of all children, cookies.

Dennis replied (my paraphrase), "I'm not getting cookies because I am good. I'm getting cookies because Mrs. Wilson is good!"

We are not blessed because we do everything right. We are blessed because He did everything right on our behalf.

The Old Covenant system is: do good, get good; or do bad, get bad.

The New Covenant system is: do good, get good; do bad, get good.

Your blessings are based on what Jesus did for you.

I am not promoting doing bad, but when you blow it, there is mercy and grace for you.

> **REVELATION 12:11**
> *"And they overcame him by the blood of the Lamb and by the word of their testimony, and they did not love their lives to the death."*

When you give testimony to God's glory, you are also saying, "God do it again in my life."

When Patti and I gave our testimony of receiving $100,000 after giving $100, financial miracles multiplied among our hearers!

- The pastor of that church received $3,000,000 to pay off their building.
- Someone else stepped up and paid for a car.
- One person received $500,000.
- Another person received $50,000,000 for a construction bid.

CHAPTER 10

Supernatural Increase Manual

PART II: REVELATION

1. The Blank Check of the Lord

"The Blank Check of the Lord" is about believing that God can give you anything you want. With man this is impossible, but with God all things are possible.

He is not a Sugar Daddy, but He is *my* Daddy and He loves me.

He already made the biggest sacrifice by sending His Son to die for me. Everything else is far less.

One day, I was sitting in my truck praying, when God gave me a vision of a blank check. I knew instantly it was the blank check of the Lord.

He gave it to me and He wanted me to use it, and I have used it many times.

In reality, God did not give you just a single blank check, or even the checkbook; but He gave His Son, Jesus. I am up to check #5000. How about you?

777 Heaven
The Kingdom of God
Not of this Earth

1936

Anytime or place

DATE

PAY TO THE ORDER OF Any of my children who ask me

$

Any amount they ask for and have need of

DOLLARS

FOR

Blood of Jesus

⑆000000186⑆ 000000529⑈ 1000

Address:

777 Heaven

The Kingdom of God

Not of this Earth

Date: Anytime or place

Pay to the order of: Any of my Children who ask Me
Amount: Any amount they ask for and have need of
Signed: By the Blood of Jesus, paid in full.

How do we cash this check? Believe in His Word and promises.

JOHN 15:7
"If you abide in Me, and My words abide in you ask what you desire, and it shall be done for you."

JOHN 15:8
"By this My Father is glorified, that you bear much fruit, so you will be My disciples."

EPHESIANS 3:20 (NIV)
"Now to Him who is able to do immeasurably more than all we ask or imagine, according to His power that is at work within us."

PHILIPPIANS 4:19
"And My God shall supply all your need according to His riches in glory by Christ Jesus."

1 JOHN 5:14-15
"Now this is the confidence that we have in Him, that if we ask anything according to His will, He hears us. And if we know that He hears us, whatever we ask, we know that we have the petitions that we have asked of Him."

2. The Court and the Justice of our God

Once, when I was wronged, I did not rise up to petition the Lord on my own behalf.

Did you know that going and praying to God based on His promises as Your provider and defender is an act of faith? To not turn to God is to rely on yourself!

We fight from a place of victory because of the cross. He wants us to approach the throne with boldness. Yes, God is a judge, but I am a son of The Judge. He is my Dad and I have favor.

When you have been wronged, pray to your loving Father who is the judge of the universe. Let your expectation come from God answering your prayers, and not man.

God's Promise of 100-fold

MATTHEW 19:29
"And everyone who has left houses or brothers or sisters or father or mother or wife or children or lands, for My name's sake, shall receive a hundredfold, and inherit eternal life."

EPHESIANS 3:20-21 (MSG)
"God can do anything, you know—far more than you could ever imagine or guess or request in your wildest dreams! He does it not by pushing us around but by working within us, His Spirit deeply and gently within us."

God spoke this to me as He was calling me to turn to Him in petition and to act as My Defender:

"Son, think higher and bigger of what is in My heart for you. If you cannot go there, you will not come into your destiny. For I am not a man that I would lie. I challenge you to believe I am this good. Blessing flows to those who dare to believe!

The Devil is impatient and he attacks first. He tips the scales of justice to bring injustice.

I want My people to petition Me on these matters. Pray and find the scriptures as if you were an attorney and study them. Come before Me. Plead your case to Me and I will pass judgment on your behalf.

Where are your petitions? How have you been wronged? State your case and I will hear.

If you do business with Me, then you will do My business.

How can you minister to others if you do not let Me minister to you? Don't be like the church of Laodicea who says, 'I have need of nothing.'

Plead your case to Me and I will pass judgment on your behalf. But if you lost everything because of Me, I will restore you one-hundred fold. This is all part of praying, 'Your kingdom come, Your will be done.'

Son, if you find it in the scriptures, it is yours. Search for wisdom and knowledge. They are true silver and gold. You will not only get these in the natural, but also so much more."

Hidden Treasures

I had a dream. In the dream, a police officer friend came to my house. It was a big house full of young people.

The officer pulled out a large flashlight and, together, we went searching through the house.

We found a wall safe in a closet and tried to open it. After many tries, we finally cracked it. Inside the safe, there were many treasures. There were gold and silver coins, diamonds, rubies, precious gemstones, anointing oil, manna, and communion wine. It was incredible!

Did you know you have a wall safe?

The Holy Spirit is your flash light, and your hidden treasures are found in the word of God.

> **ISAIAH 45:2-3**
> *"I will go before you, and make the crooked*
> *places straight; I will break in pieces the gates*
> *of bronze and cut the bars of iron. I will give*
> *you the treasures of darkness, and hidden*
> *riches of secret places, that you may know*
> *that I, the Lord, who call you by your name,*
> *Am the God of Israel."*

To know God is to have unlimited wealth and prosperity in everything. God has given you the keys to the Kingdom so that whatever you bind on earth will be bound in heaven, and whatever you lose on earth will be loosed in heaven. God told me, "You are my son and I will bring great wealth through your hands, and it will not stop."

3. The Parable of the Persistent Widow

Persistence in prayer is important because there is resistance. Patti and I have prayed for about two months for several breakthroughs, while some breakthroughs have taken many years of faithful praying.

When you continue to pray over a period of time, you are breaking down the resistance.

I prayed five years for a boss's salvation. Because he was not open to it, I never got to share the Gospel with him. When I was leaving that job, I asked his brother to keep praying for him, and urged him to continue praying until it came to pass. He agreed.

Two years later, it happened!

> **LUKE 18:1-8**
> *"Then He spoke a parable to them that men always ought to pray and not lose heart, saying: 'There was in a certain city a judge who did not fear God nor regard man. Now there was a widow in that city; and she came to him, saying, and 'Get justice for me from my adversary.' And he would not for a while; but afterward he said within himself, 'Though I do not fear God nor regard man, yet because this widow troubles me I will avenge her, lest by her continual coming she weary me.'"*

Are we asking, seeking and knocking?

God says, "I will avenge her."

> *"Then the Lord said, 'Hear what the unjust judge said. And shall God not avenge His own*

elect who cry out day and night to Him,
though He bears long with them I tell you that
He will avenge them speedily. Nevertheless,
when the Son of Man comes, will He really
find faith on the earth?'"

Faith on the earth is His own elect, who cry out day and night to Him.

- Are you bringing your petitions before God like this?

- Do you believe the Bible?

- Do you believe that God parted the Red Sea for His people to cross it?

- That He healed the ten lepers?

- Do you believe in miracles?

- Will you expect to see miracles in your own life today?

4. The Prayer of Jabez

I love the prayer of Jabez because he simply wanted to be blessed, and God answered that request.

No one wants to be a loser. We all have a desire to be fruitful.

1 CHRONICLES 4:9-10
"Now Jabez was more honorable than his brothers. And his mother called his name Jabez, saying, 'Because I bore him in pain.'"

How was Jabez more honorable? His name means, "because I bore him in pain."

Jabez knew he had caused pain and he did not like it. Therefore, Jabez dared to ask, "…that I may not cause pain."

Jabez honored God by coming to Him and asked God to do something for him. This pleases God.

HEBREWS 11:6
"But without faith it is impossible to please Him, for he who comes to God must believe that He is, and that He is a rewarder of those who diligently seek Him."

Jabez called on the God of Israel, not looking to man but to God for his blessing:

"Oh, that You would bless me indeed…"
This is the very heart of God to bring us into all the blessings.

"…and enlarge my territory…"
Pray specifically for the area of life where you want the breakthrough, and do not stop till it is done.

"…that Your hand would be with me…"
You are one with God because He lives inside of you; therefore, He is always there to guide and protect you.

"...and that You would keep me from evil, that I may not cause pain!"

We are to love one another. Our endeavors should not cause harm or pain to others but bring healing into the earth.

"...So, God granted him what he requested."

- God only answers prayers that are aligned with His will.

- God granted Jabez' request.

- It is God's will to bless you.

5. Speak to the Rock

NUMBERS 20:8
"Take the rod; you and your brother Aaron gather the congregation together. Speak to the rock before their eyes, and it will yield its water; thus you shall bring water for them out of the rock, and give drink to the congregation and their animals."

"Speak to the rock," God told Moses. But as the story goes, Moses did not speak to the rock but chose to strike it.

Previously, Moses had been instructed by God to strike the rock to bring the people water. Historically, this was not heard of. People traveling through the wilderness find water hidden within the rocks?

Yet, this time, God was asking Moses only to speak to the rock. God was asking Moses to trust Him.

By beating the rock, he was angry and showed trust in his own strength rather than God's.

Because Moses lost his cool and did not trust God in this, he was not permitted to enter the Promised Land.

We, too, could fail to enter our Promised Land if we do not speak to the Rock. The Rock is Jesus Christ, and He was struck (beaten) so that we could have a right relationship with God. Now, all we have to do is enjoy relationship with Christ and speak to Him.

Once I had a minister ask me to give a certain amount to his ministry. He said it would unlock heaven. So, I asked the Lord about it. This was my Father's response:

"Son, heaven is already unlocked through my Son Jesus, but giving always activates the release of funds. My servant needs funds. He is an apostle. He will use it for the Kingdom. You cannot lose giving to the Lord and the work of the Lord. You cannot out-give Me.

In the Old Testament, people tried to open heaven by fasting and praying. In the New Testament, My love for My Son opened the heavens when I said, 'This is my beloved Son in whom I am well pleased.'

Now you are the son and heaven is open for you because of the cross. Just as with Moses who only needed to strike the rock once and the second time ask; so My Son, your Rock, was beaten once, and to get what you need, you need only to ask."

6. Words from God about Great Wealth

These are words that have shaped my destiny and have released wealth into my life, and if you dare to believe them, they will be God's Words to you, too.

> **HEBREWS 8:10-11**
> *"This is the covenant I will establish with the people of Israel after that time, declares the Lord. I will put my laws in their minds and write them on their hearts. I will be their God, and they will be my people. No longer will they teach their neighbor, or say to one another, 'Know the Lord,' because they will all know me, from the least of them to the greatest."*

God put His laws in our hearts. His Spirit speaks to us inwardly and teaches us. Because God speaks to us, we know Him.

> **1 JOHN 2:27**
> *"As for you, the anointing you received from Him remains in you, and you do not need anyone to teach you. But as His anointing teaches you about all things and as that anointing is real, not counterfeit—just as it has taught you, remain in Him."*

These are things God spoke to me that you can take for yourself. I dare you to believe!

- *I am making you a steward over My finances. Give everything you own to Me and take care of it well.*

- *Your relationship with Me will bring everything in your life that you desire. I am the best investment one could ever have.*

- *Men go after silver and gold, but I am your investment that will pay off in every way. For I know your heart's desire and I will fulfill it. I delight in blessing you.*

- *This is all part of praying, "Your kingdom come, Your will be done." If you find it in the scriptures, it is yours. Search for wisdom like you would for silver and gold, and you will not only get these in the natural but also so much more.*

- *The investments you have made, for which people criticized you, the Lord says, "Tonight, I breathe life into them. I am turning them around."*

- *The Lord says, "I am going to show you some witty inventions, too."*

- *Don't I own the cattle on a thousand hills? I also own the hills that the cattle are on and I know where the gold and silver lie. I also know your address.*

- *Your debt will be paid off just because you spent time with Me.*

- *Anything that is unfruitful and frustrating is you. Anything that is fruitful is Me!*

- *What are you looking at? (I was at the gym standing in front of a mirror flexing my muscles). If you will spend the time with Me that you do in the gym, I will put gold into your heart.*

- *They did not receive the blessing. They did not know the goodness of God in the land of the living. But you do, so I am going to cause you to lead.*

- *You are receiving special favor, the Anointing of Distinction, deeper revelation of grace and tremendous breakthrough in finances.*

- *You have turned a corner to believe in the blank check of the Lord. Believe that I will give you what you want, and not just what you need. This is My heart for you.*

- *I am blessing you like nothing you have ever experienced. Pray for the $1,000,000 and I will bring it. Then, pray for $10,000,000, and I will bring it. (God, I ask for the $1,000,000 and I ask for $10,000,000).*

- *Yes, there will be people that will judge your heart. This provokes Me to give to you even more. Son, you are a millionaire and now you are a billionaire, just because I said it.*

- *Judgment of the King: request granted. You are My Son and I will bring great wealth through your hands, and it will not stop.*

- *Study My word on finances, for that is a place I want to bless you in.*

7. Seven Steps to Prayer

The seven steps to prayer are not a formula, but a guide to understanding a few crucial elements of fervent prayers.

First, you must know what you want.

Then, you must ask and discern whether your desire is aligned with God's heart.

Once you know your desire is aligned with God's, then you need to ask for it; be certain that you have what you have asked for; and thank the Lord in advance.

1. Decide what you want from God.

    a) Make a list.

    b) Know that what you want is already in your heart.

    c) Believe. Do not be double minded. (James 1:2-8)

2. Read His promises in scripture.

    a) The Word will always confirm whatever is His will, so pray according to the Word.

    b) Understand that anything found in the scriptures belongs to you. Deuteronomy 29:29 says: "The secret things belong to the LORD our God, but those things which are revealed belong to us and to our children forever, that we *may do all the words of this law.*"

3. Ask God for things you need. Pray, and be specific. If you need an increase of $1000 in your monthly income, ask Him for $1000. I have seen Him do this in less than a week. This is no problem for God who owns the universe.

> **MATTHEW 7:7-11**
> *"Ask and it will be given to you; seek and you will find; knock and the door will be opened to you. For everyone who asks receives; the one who seeks finds; and to the one who knocks, the door will be opened."*

*"Which of you, if your son asks for bread, will
give him a stone? Or if he asks for a fish, will
give him a snake? If you, then, though you are
evil, know how to give good gifts to your
children, how much more will your Father in
heaven give good gifts to those who ask
Him!"*

4. Use the scriptures for prayer and petitions.

    a) Pray the scriptures.

    b) What He has done for others, He will do for
    you.

5. Proclaim the scriptures.

    a) Stand with confidence and declare His
    Word.

    b) Romans 4:17 reminds us that when God
    speaks, He "calls into being things that are
    not." His Word is creative. Speak it!

    c) When you speak His Words aloud, you
    command God's will to be done on earth as
    it is in heaven.

6. Believe you have them, because you ask.

    a) Refuse to doubt.

1 JOHN 5:14-15 SAYS
*"Now this is the confidence that we have in
Him, that if we ask anything according to His
will, He hears us. And if we know that He
hears us, whatever we ask, we know that we
have the petitions that we have asked of Him."*

7. Praise and immediately thank God for answering prayer.

    a) Before you see it with your eyes, believe it.

b) We walk by faith, not by sight.

c) Worship Him and celebrate the victory.

d) Know that God will answer prayer, but it may look different than you expected.

e) Expect God to blow your mind.

8. We Ask Too Small

We don't ask for ourselves enough when God wants to do more for us than we think. We have to remind ourselves that God made everything and nothing is too big to ask for. We ask for crumbs like God is a stingy man. It is not His will to be stingy, but instead, ask Him for the seven course meal.

I remember being at a men's prayer meeting and seeing Jesus standing with his arms folded. He said, "Ye of little faith. I have so much more for you, you ask too small."

Years ago, a famous golfer was invited by the king of Saudi Arabia to play in a golf tournament. He accepted the invitation, and the Saudi king flew his private jet over to the United States to pick him up. They played golf for several days, and had a good time. As the golfer was getting on the plane to return to the United States, the king stopped him and said, "I want to give you a gift for coming all this way and making this time so special. Anything you want. What could I get you?"

Ever the gentleman, the golfer replied, "Oh, please; do not get me anything. You've been a gracious host. I've had a wonderful time. I couldn't ask for anything more."

The king was adamant. He said, "No, I insist on giving you something so you will always remember your journey to our country. If you do not receive a gift I will be offended."

When the golfer realized that the king was resolute, he said, "Okay, fine. I collect golf clubs. Why don't you give me a golf club?"

As the golfer was boarding the plane on his way home he couldn't help but wonder what kind of golf club the king was going to give him. He imagined that it might be a solid gold putter with his name engraved on it. Or maybe it would be a sand wedge studded with diamonds and jewels. After all, this would be a gift from the oil-rich king of Saudi-Arabia.

A few weeks after the golfer returned home to the Unites States he received a certified letter from the king of Saudi Arabia. The U.S. professional thought that rather strange. Where's my golf club? He wondered. He opened the envelope, and to his surprise, inside he discovered a deed to a five-hundred acre golf course in America.

Remember you are asking the God who makes everything in the heavens and the earth. If you are asking Him just to make it each week, you are asking too small. In fact, it may even be offensive to God that you ask for such small things.

HAGGAI 2:8
*"The silver is Mine, and the gold is Mine,'
says the Lord of hosts."*

The Word Shall Not Return Void

ISAIAH 55:10-11 NIV

"As the rain and the snow come down from heaven, and do not return to it without watering the earth and making it bud and flourish, so that it yields seed for the sower and bread for the eater, so is my word that goes out from my mouth: It will not return to me empty, but will accomplish what I desire and achieve the purpose for which I sent it."

I have told many people, now including you, about the thousand-fold blessings Patti and I received- the houses, the restoration in family, and all of the incredible favor God gave to us as we sought first the Kingdom.

As we testify to God's works and share the Gospel, Patti and I have been blessed to watch as God's Word accomplishes the purpose for which He sent it. You heard how we once had the privilege of joining Dr. Gershom who was speaking at All Nations Church, and we had the opportunity to share the testimony of our great financial breakthrough.

Then, we prayed that this church would receive the $1.2-million they needed to pay off their church building. Four nights later, they received an anonymous gift of $3-million.

My friends, this happens all the time. Whenever we minister the word concerning supernatural increase, sharing our testimonies and teaching from the scriptures, people experience financial breakthroughs.

Now that we've shared it with you, I prophesy the same over you.

Be expectant!

Listen for the guidance of the Holy Spirit. When you pray, believe you have received it, and it will be yours.

Before walking in all of this breakthrough, the Lord had encouraged me, "Study my word on finances. I want to bless you and Patti in finances like you've never thought possible."

He then led me into His Word regarding finances, which I've joyfully shared with you here. It is our sincerest desire and expectation that you will walk in God's grace for miraculous provision and fulfillment, and that you will bring Him great glory and pleasure in doing so.

God also lead me to create a manual on supernatural increase to help you activate these truths and walk in them quickly.

If you haven't already, I encourage you to purchase our *The Book on Supernatural Increase Manual*, created to help you put your faith to action so that you can walk in the mind-blowing inheritance God has always planned for you. I bless you to receive from this teaching as much as I have, and even more.

About the
Author

For ordering information, upcoming events, new book
releases, speaking opportunities or to contact Jeff, visit
JPWatson.org

Jeff Watson, together with his wife Patti, empower others to find the grace and ability to succeed. Jeff has traveled the globe bringing hope and equipping others in financial success. As a visionary and business growth specialist, Jeff built his own successful construction company and investment portfolio. He is a gifted minister and works with his local church community to equip, encourage, and empower their people. He believes in the gospel of grace and his insights come from learning to trust the Lord in all things. He lives to see the lives of people transformed and changed forever. Go from ordinary to extraordinary!

Additional Resources

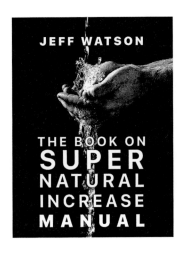

Be sure to get the companion study guide *The Book on Supernatural Increase Manual*. It was created to help you further put your faith to action so that you can walk in the mind-blowing inheritance God has always planned for you. It is available on our website:

JPWatson.org